WEDDING MUSIC FOR VIOLIN AND VIOLA

by Scott Staidle

SCORE

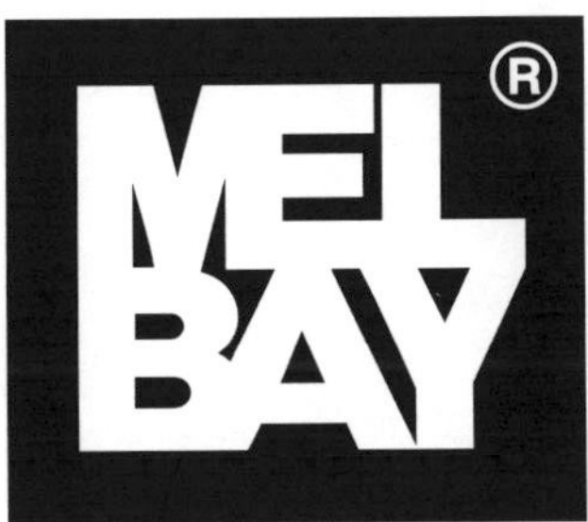

WWW.MELBAY.COM

Preface

This book, *Wedding Music for Violin and Viola*, includes 14 selections that are favorites for weddings, recitals, parties and receptions. New adaptations of these arrangements allow each musician to share melodic, harmonic and accompanying elements. These duets are well suited for intermediate to advanced musicians and include bowings, fingerings, articulations and dynamics.

ABOUT THE AUTHOR

Scott Staidle is a first violinist with the Louisville Orchestra. He has arranged the music for various orchestral concerts featuring Mel Tillis, Bryan White, Sondre Lerche and others. He also has arranged and orchestrated for the band Days of the New. As an orchestral violinist, Scott has performed with an array of artists including Ray Charles, Aretha Franklin, Glen Campbell, Ella Fitzgerald, Burt Bacharach, Henry Mancini, The Temptations, The Four Tops, America, Doc Severinsen, John Williams, Pavarotti, Itzhak Perlman, Yo-Yo Ma, Edgar Meyer, Bela Fleck, Andrea Bocelli and many others. Also, he performed on the "No Quarter" tour with Robert Plant and Jimmy Page.

Contents

Air in "D"
for Violin and Viola

Score

J. S. Bach
Arr. Scott Staidle

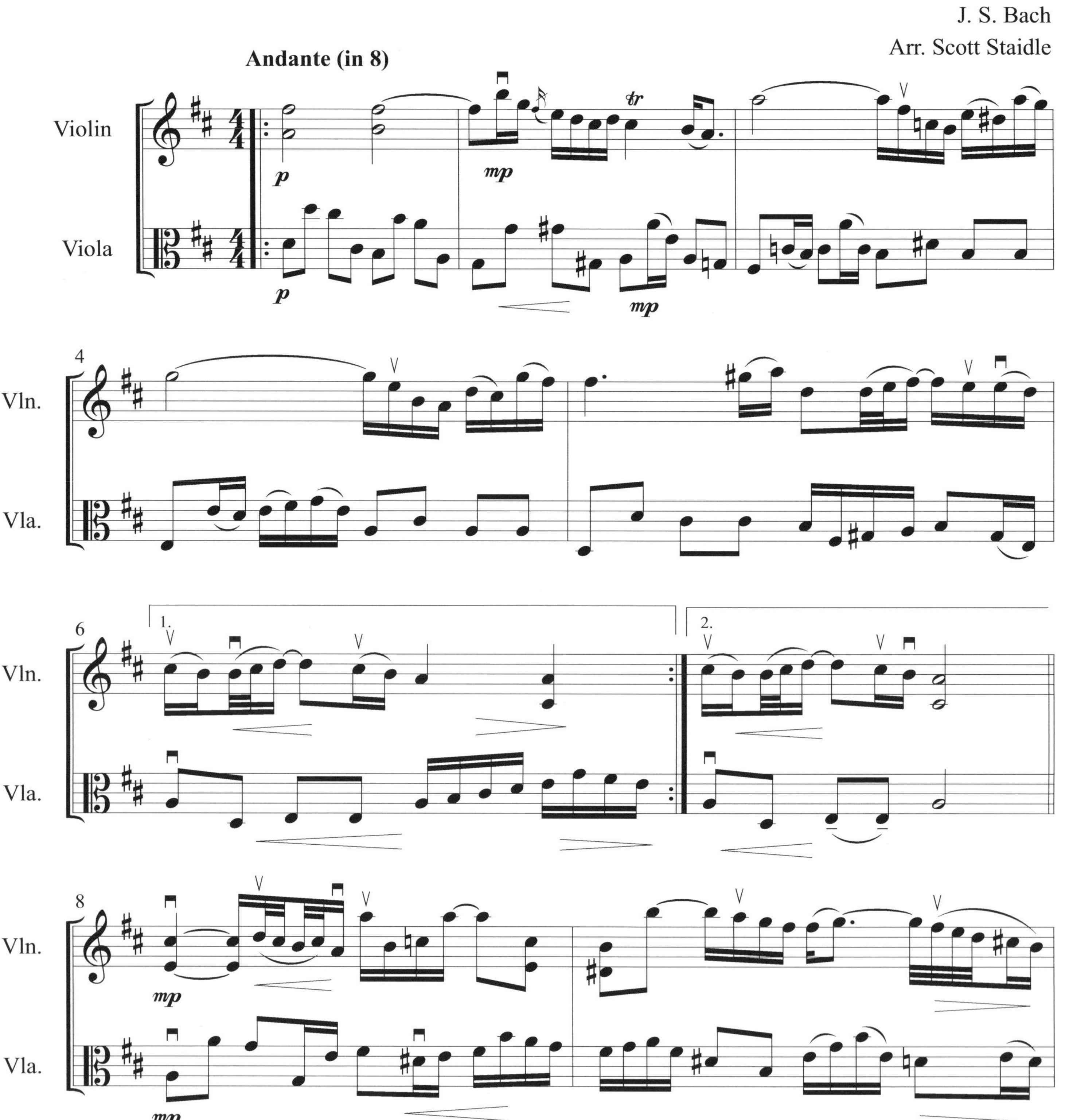

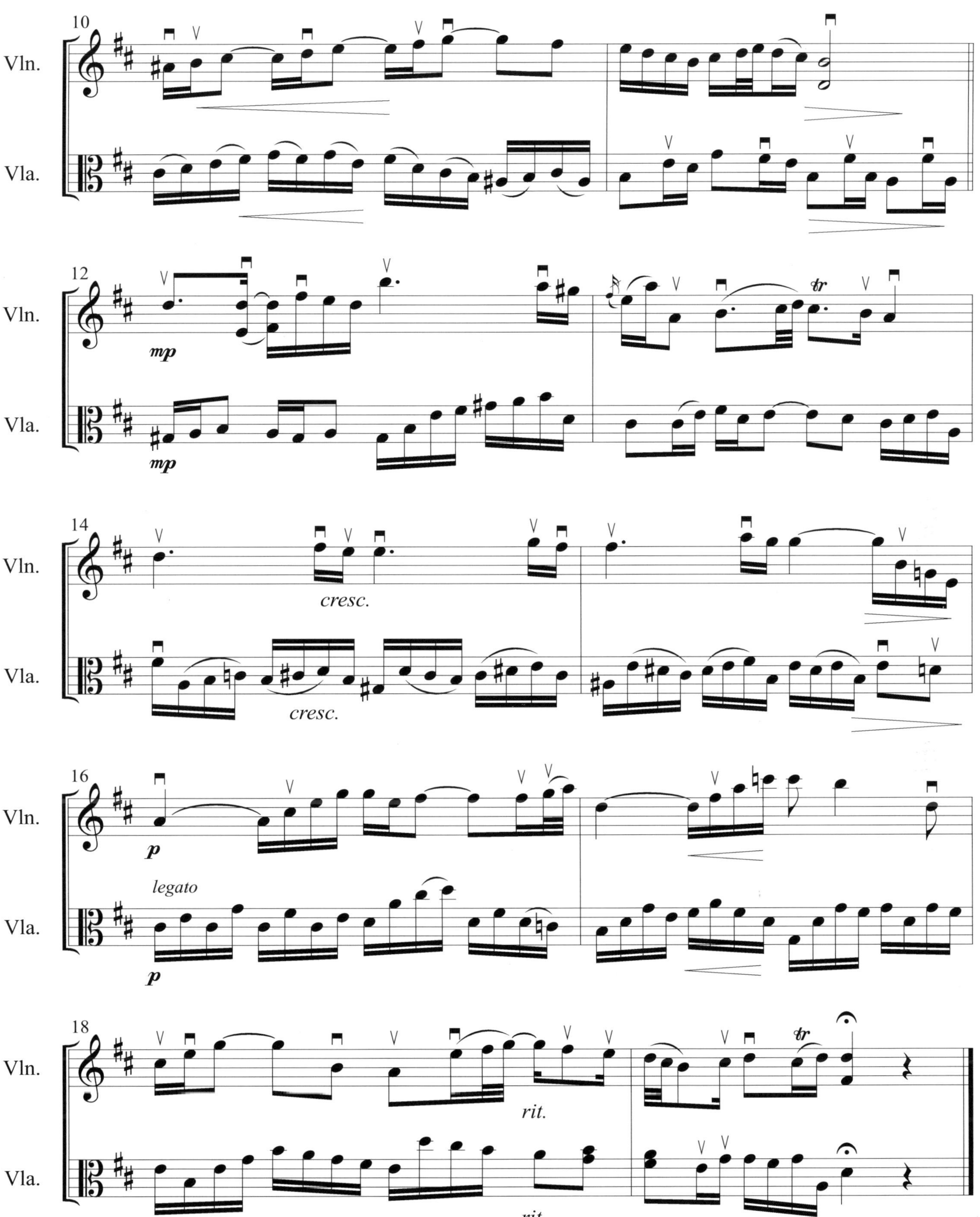
10
Vln.
Vla.
12
mp
mp
14
cresc.
cresc.
16
p
legato
p
18
rit.
rit.

Allegro
for Violin and Viola

Score

J. H. Fiocco
Arr. Scott Staidle

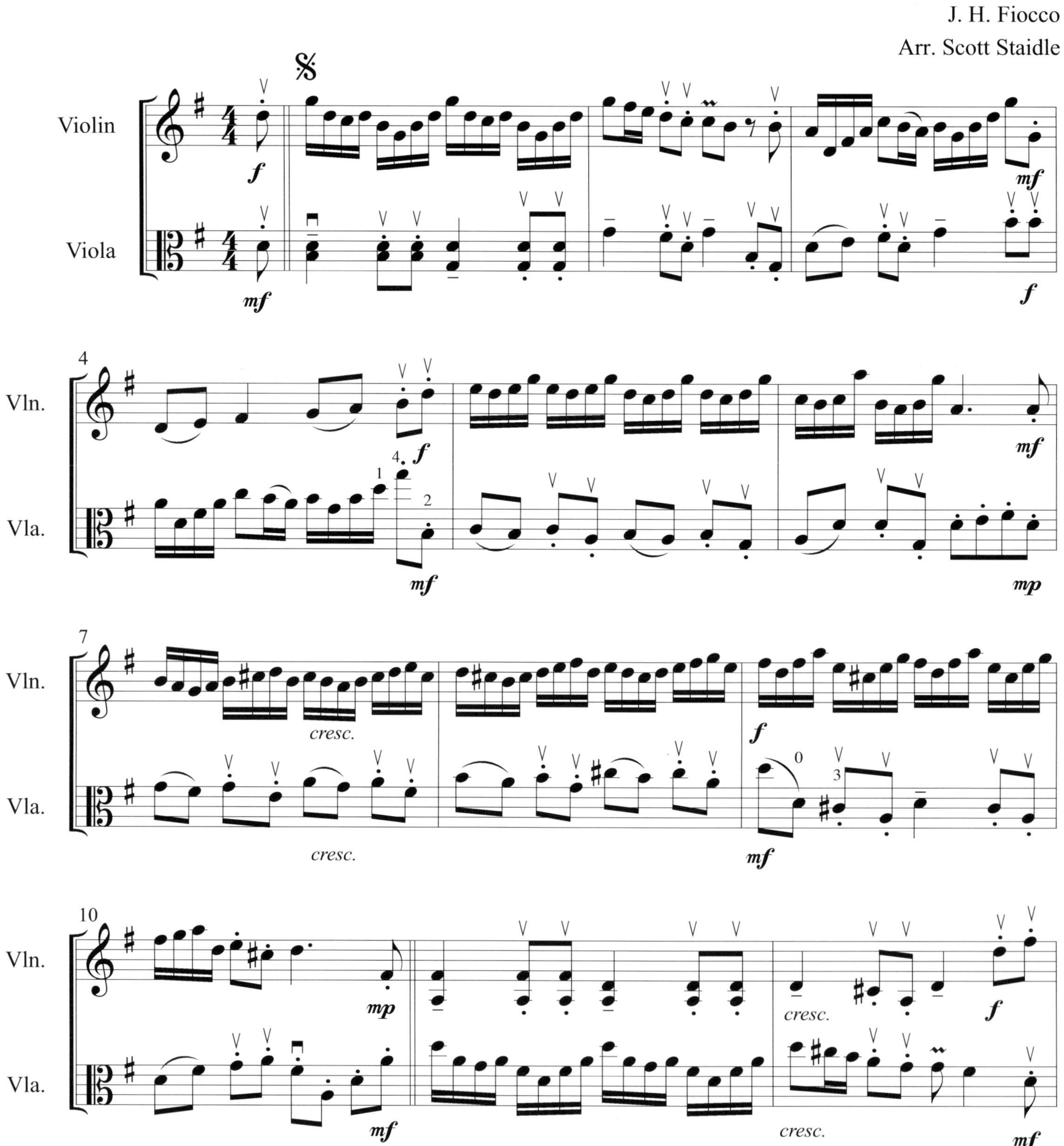

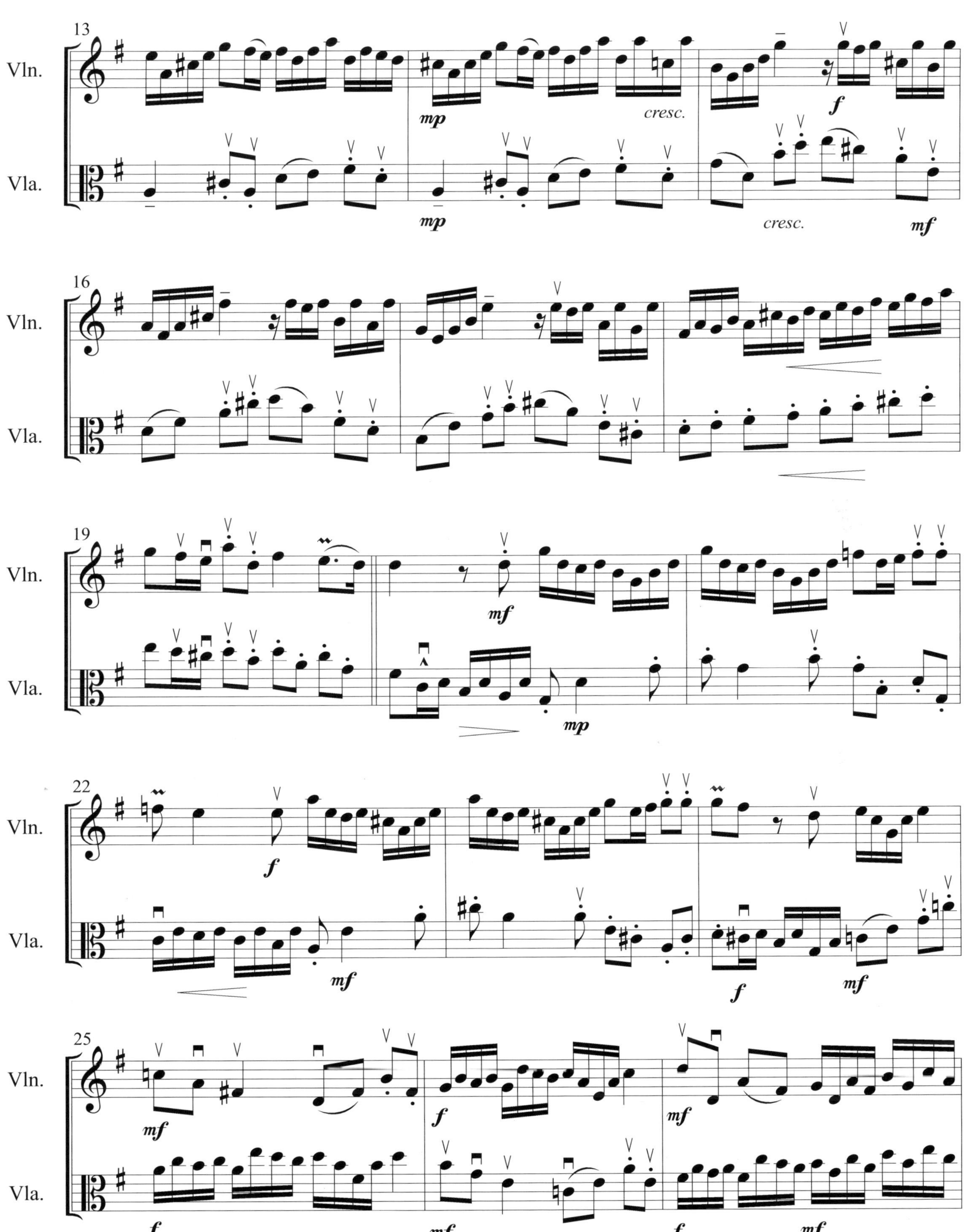
13
Vln.
Vla.
mp
cresc.
f
mf
16
19
22
25

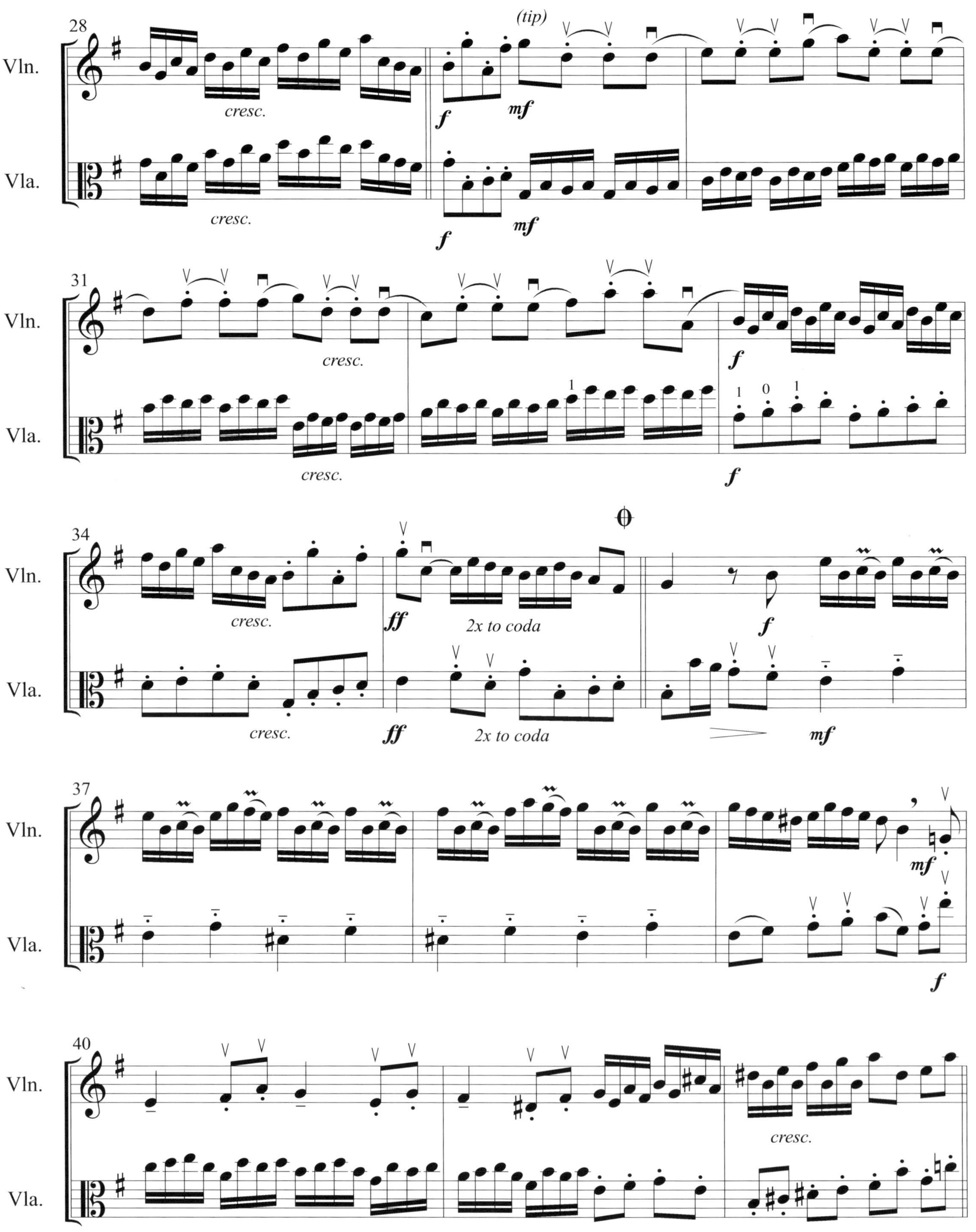
28
Vln.
Vla.
cresc.
(tip)
f
mf
31
cresc.
f
1 0 1
34
2x to coda
ff
37
mf
40

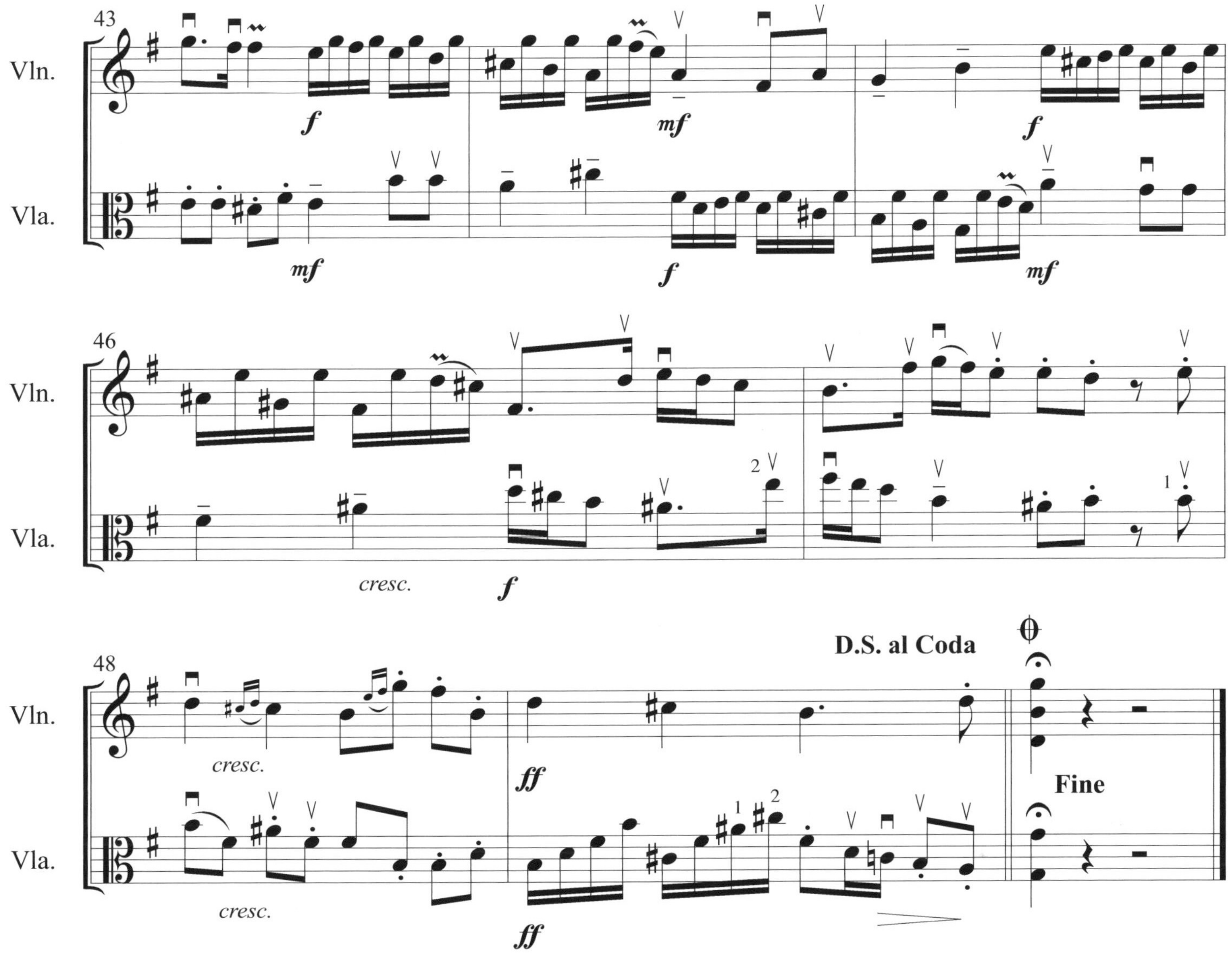
43
Vln.
Vla.
f
mf
f
mf
f
mf
46
cresc.
f
D.S. al Coda
48
cresc.
ff
Fine
cresc.
ff

Amazing Grace
for Violin and Viola

Score

Traditional
Arr. Scott Staidle

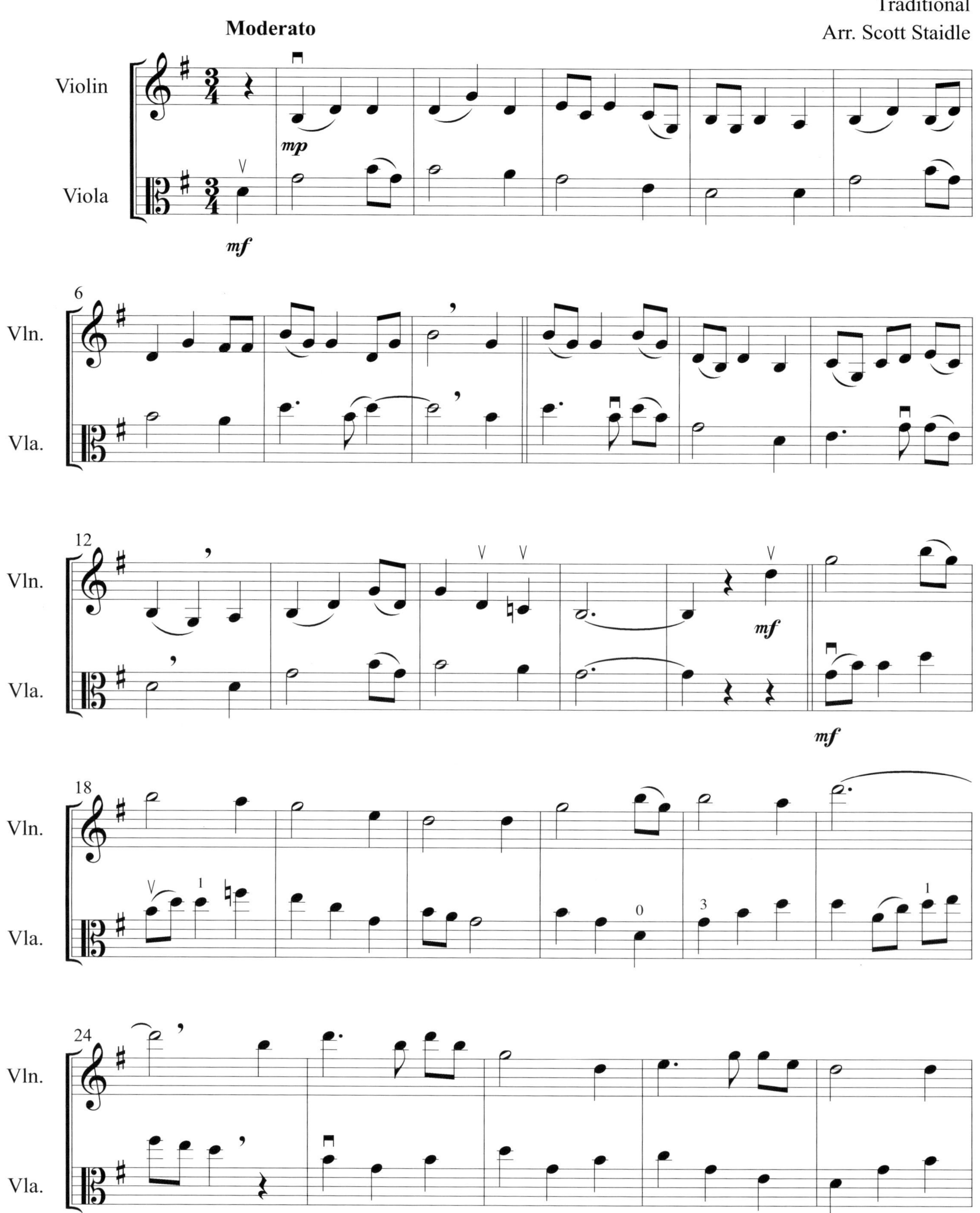

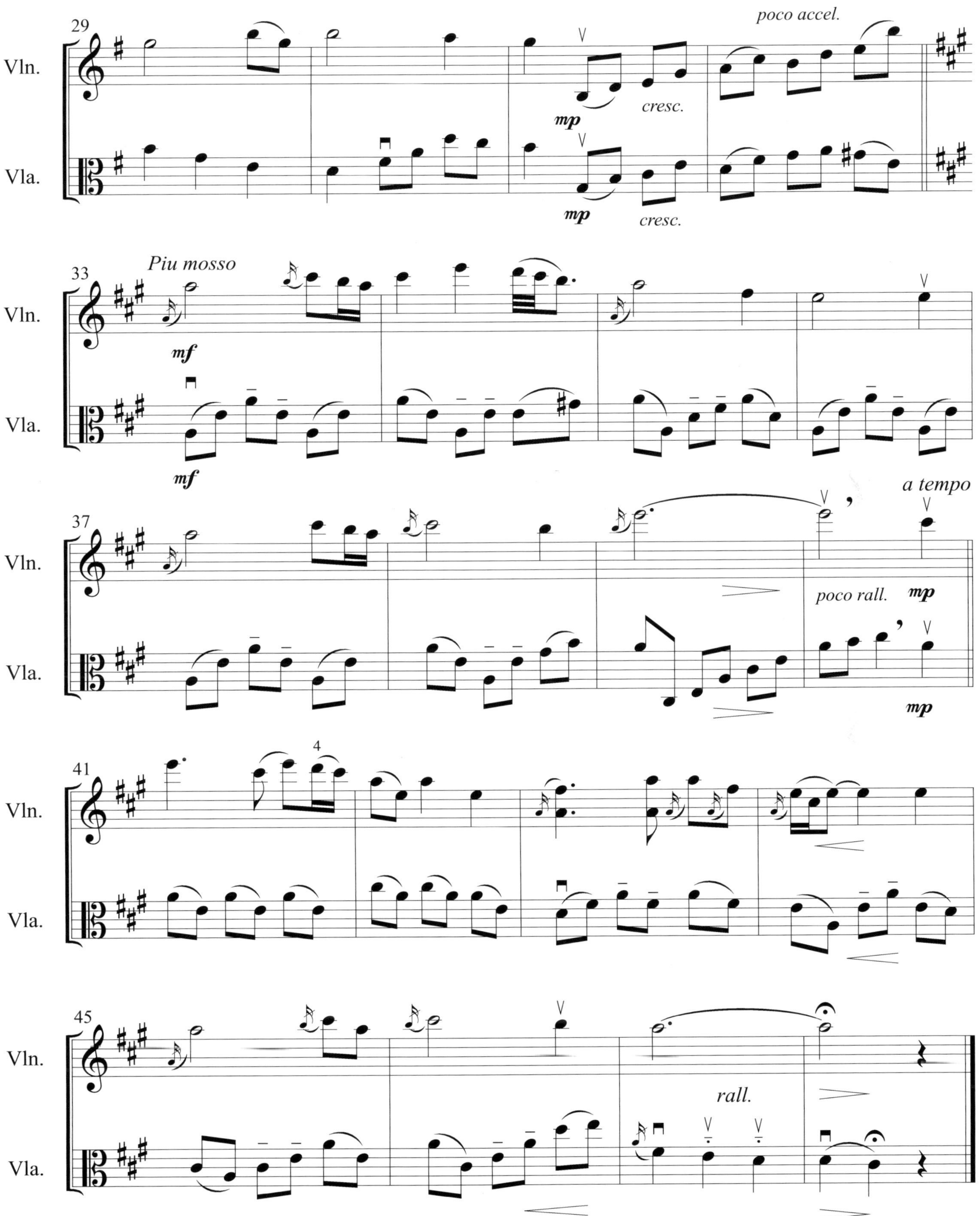
29
Vln.
Vla.
poco accel.
mp
cresc.
mp
cresc.
33
Piu mosso
mf
mf
37
a tempo
poco rall.
mp
mp
41
4
45
rall.

Jesu, Joy of Man's Desiring

for Violin and Viola

Score

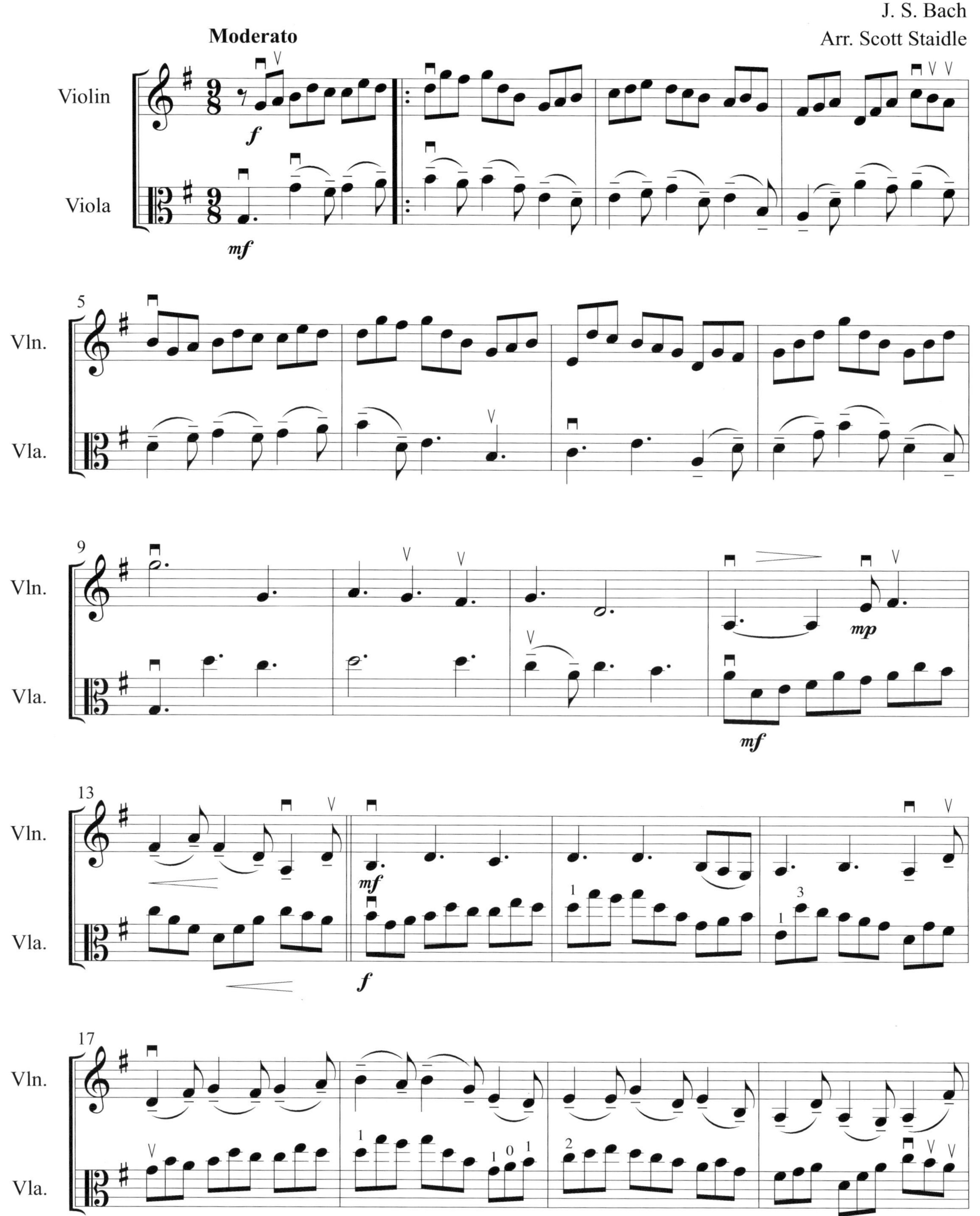

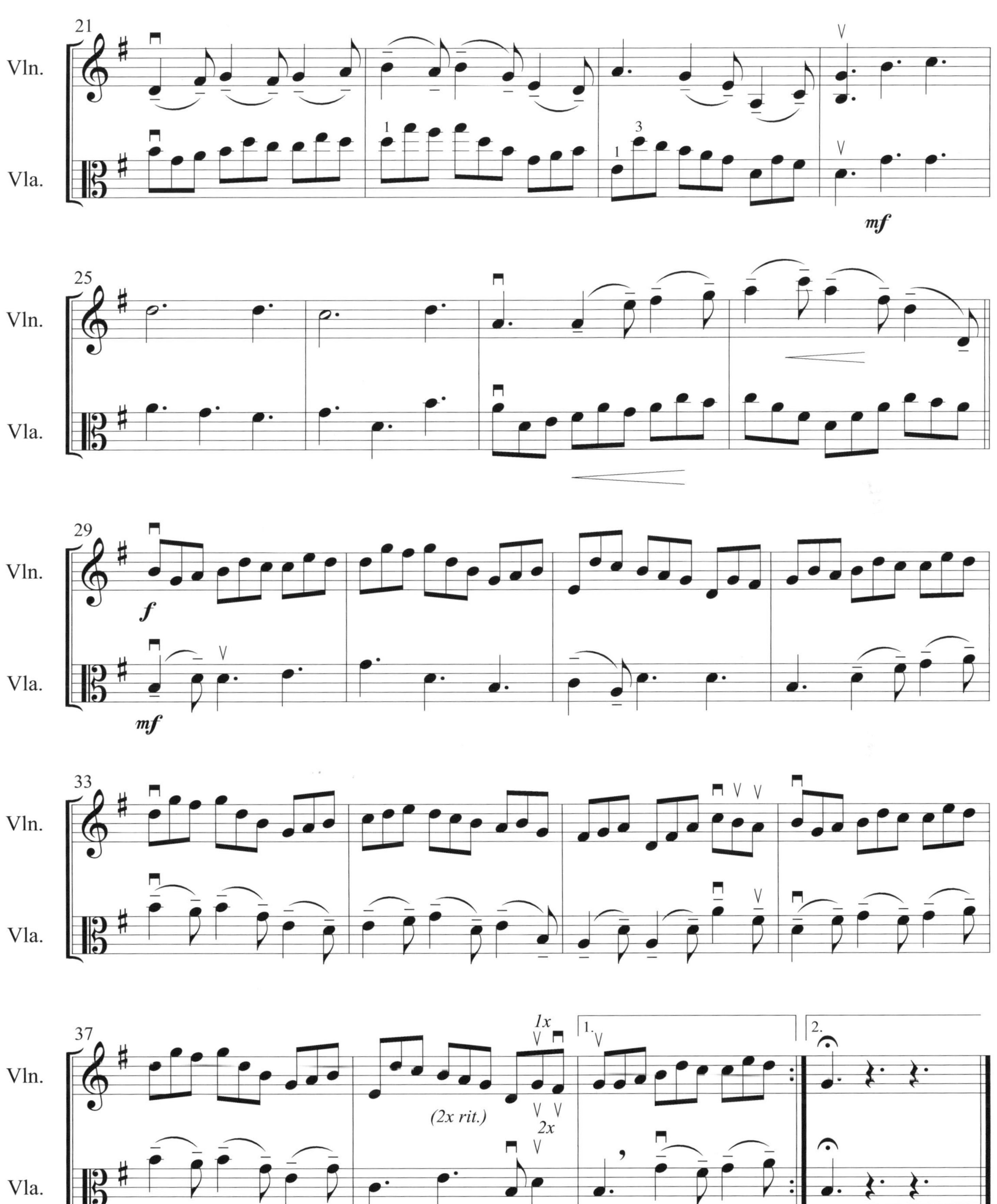
21
Vln.
Vla.
1
1
3
mf
25
29
f
mf
33
37
1x
(2x rit.)
2x
1.
2.

Kanon
for Violin and Viola

Score

J. Pachelbel
Arr. Scott Staidle

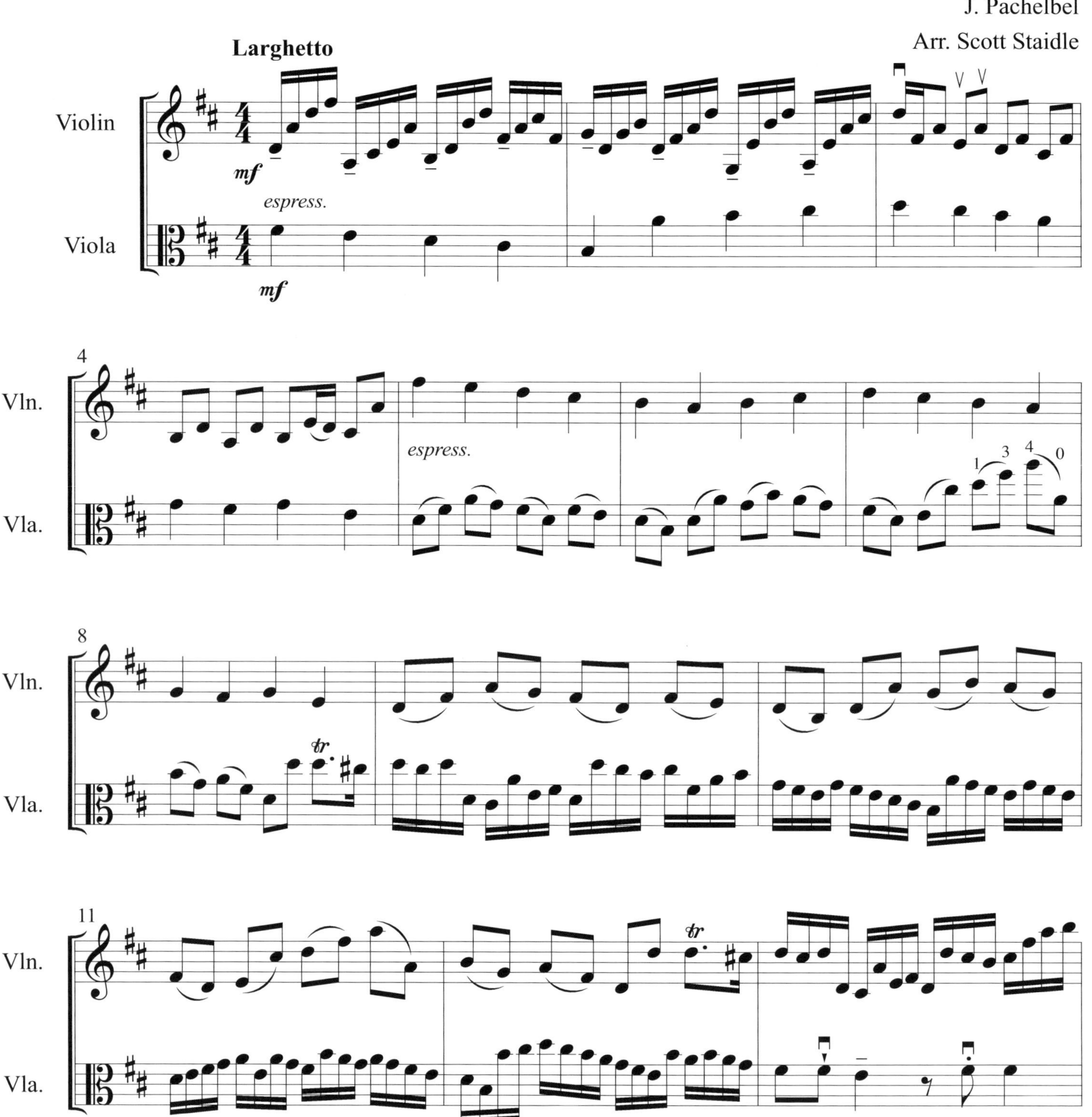

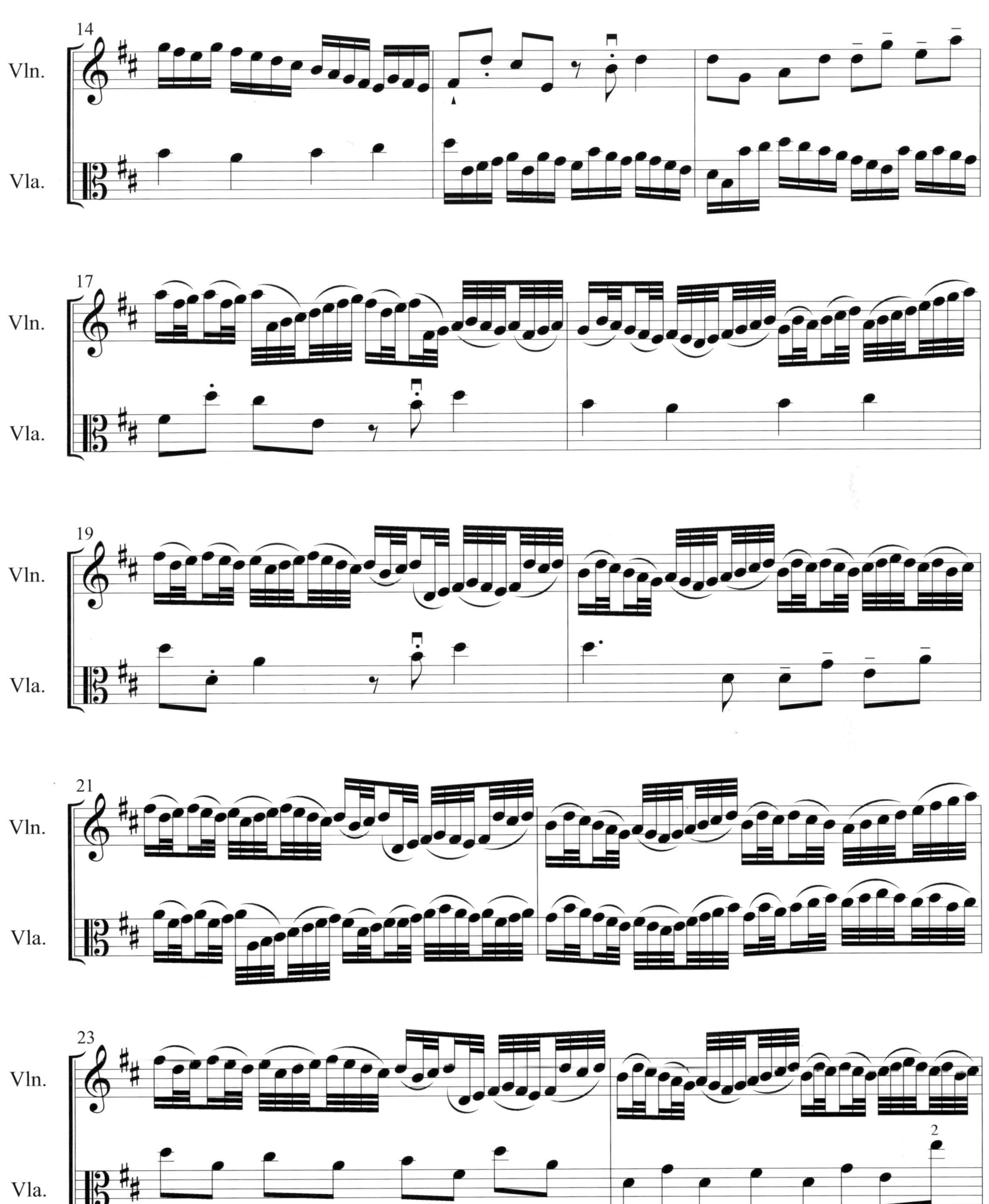
14
Vln.
Vla.
17
Vln.
Vla.
19
Vln.
Vla.
21
Vln.
Vla.
23
Vln.
Vla.
2

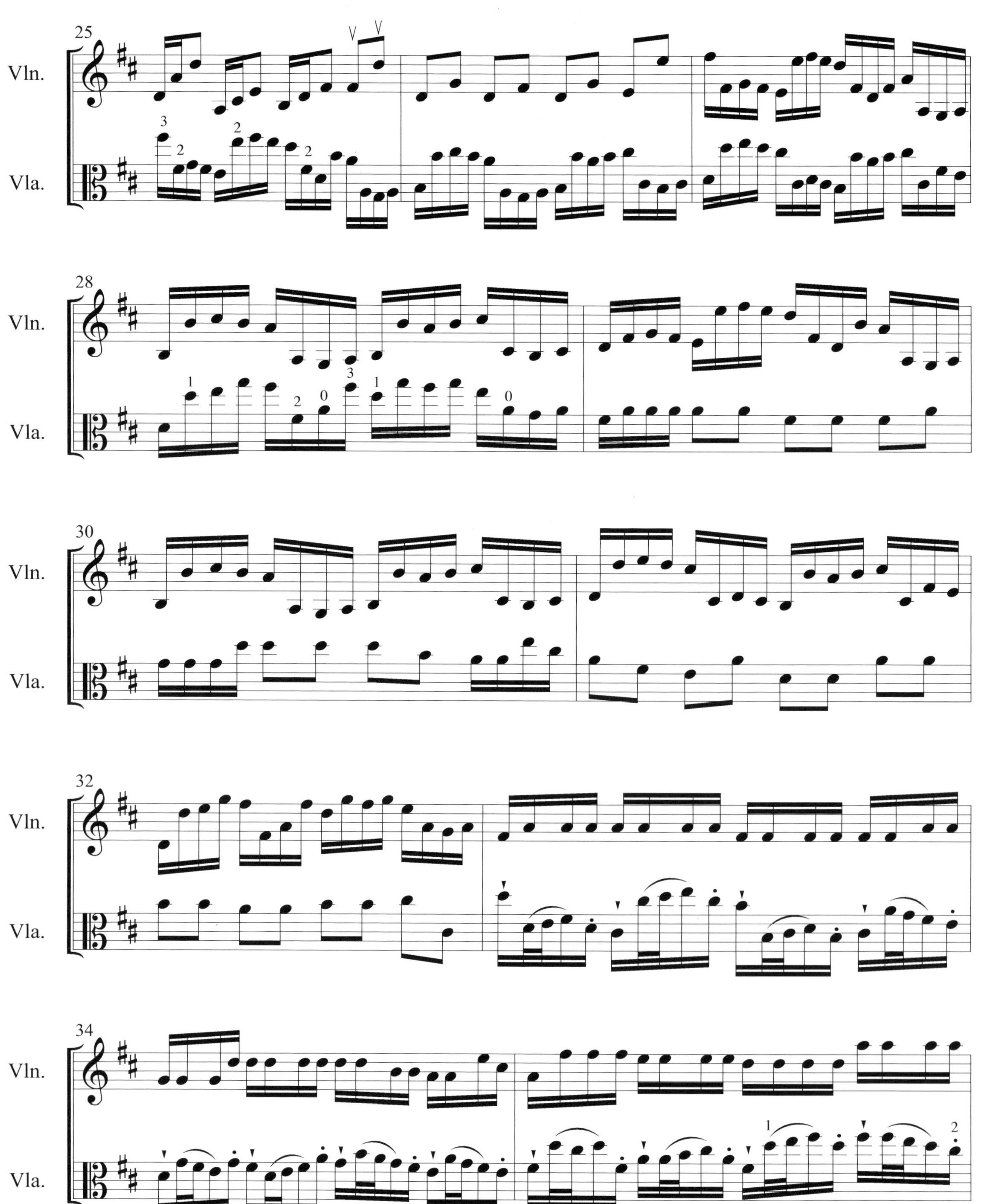
25
Vln.
Vla.
28
Vln.
Vla.
30
Vln.
Vla.
32
Vln.
Vla.
34
Vln.
Vla.

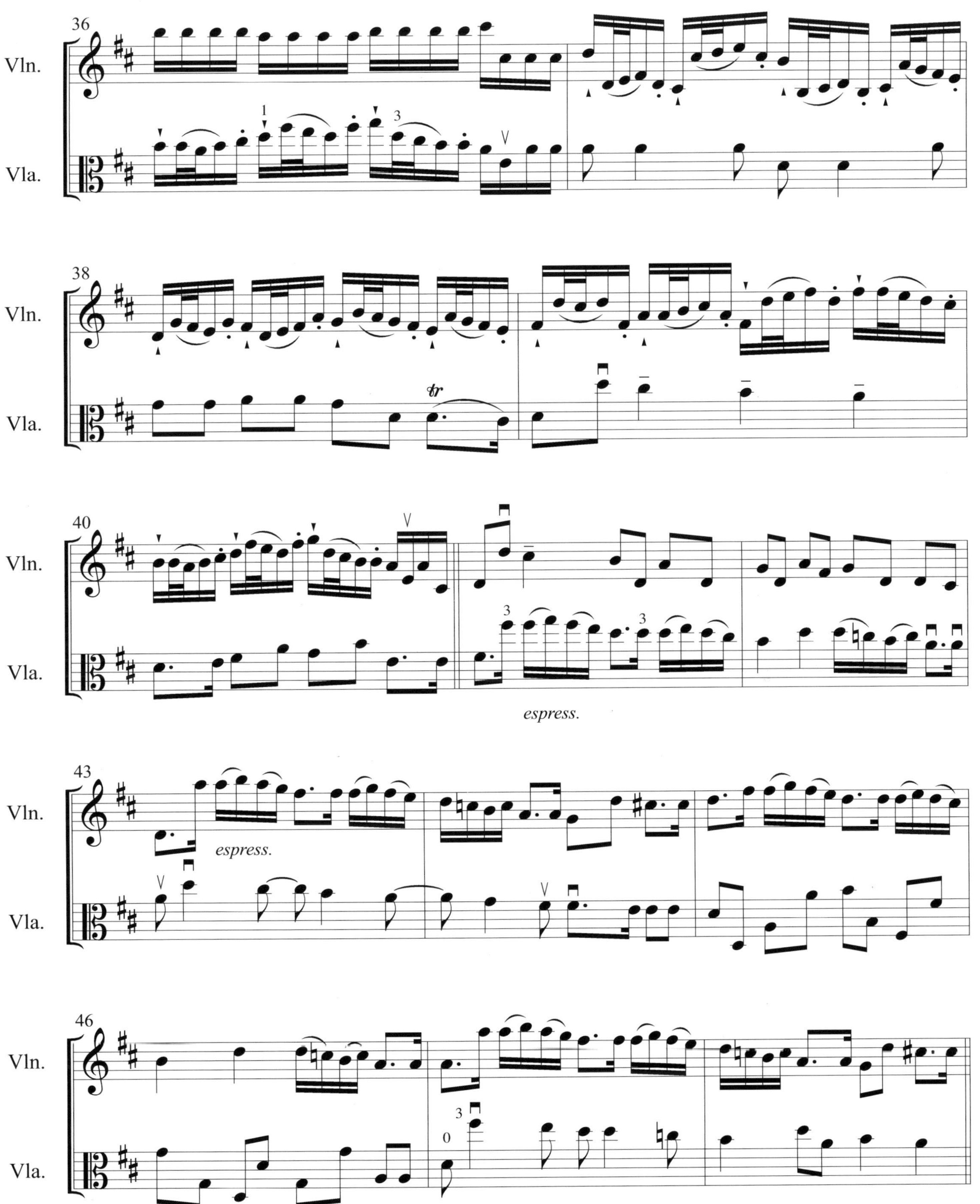
36
Vln.
Vla.
38
Vln.
Vla.
40
Vln.
Vla.
espress.
43
Vln.
espress.
Vla.
46
Vln.
Vla.

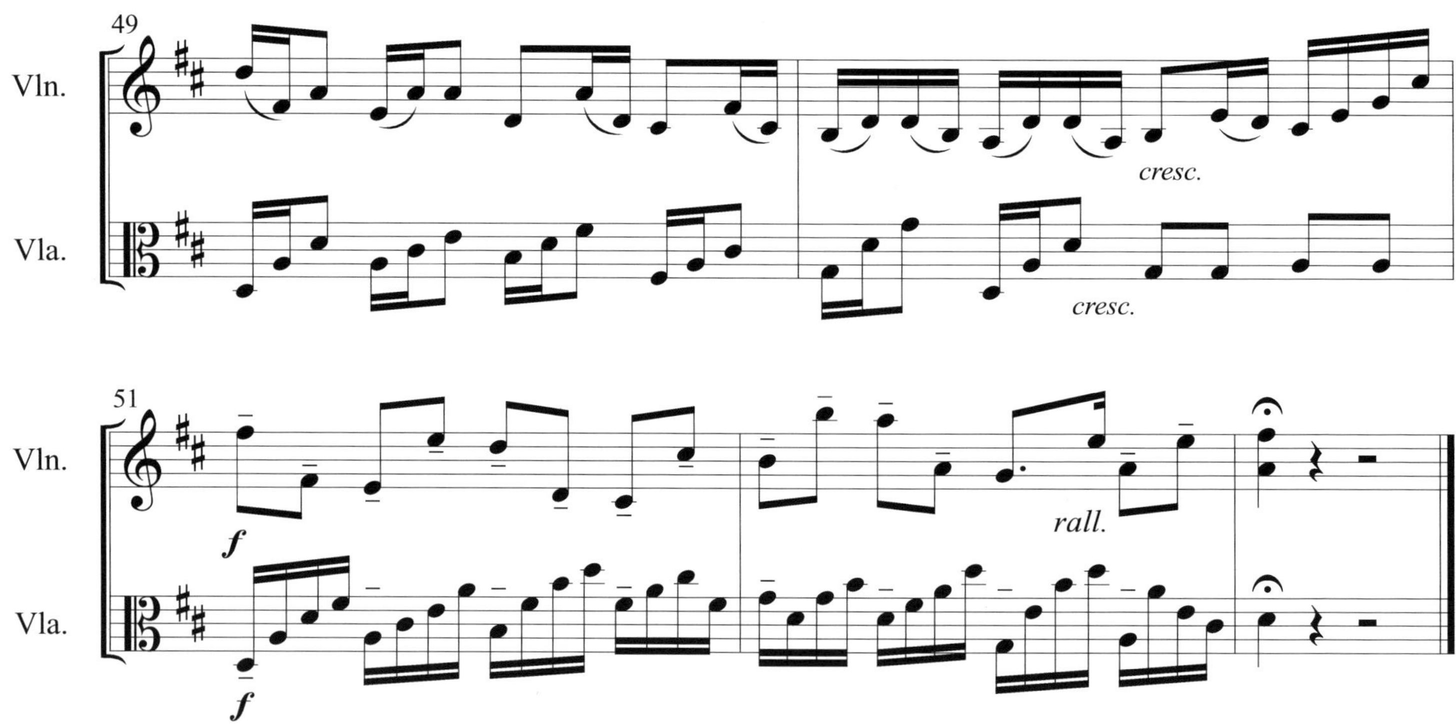

49
Vln.
Vla.
cresc.
cresc.
51
Vln.
Vla.
f
f
rall.

Bridal Chorus
for Violin and Viola

R. Wagner
Arr. Scott Staidle

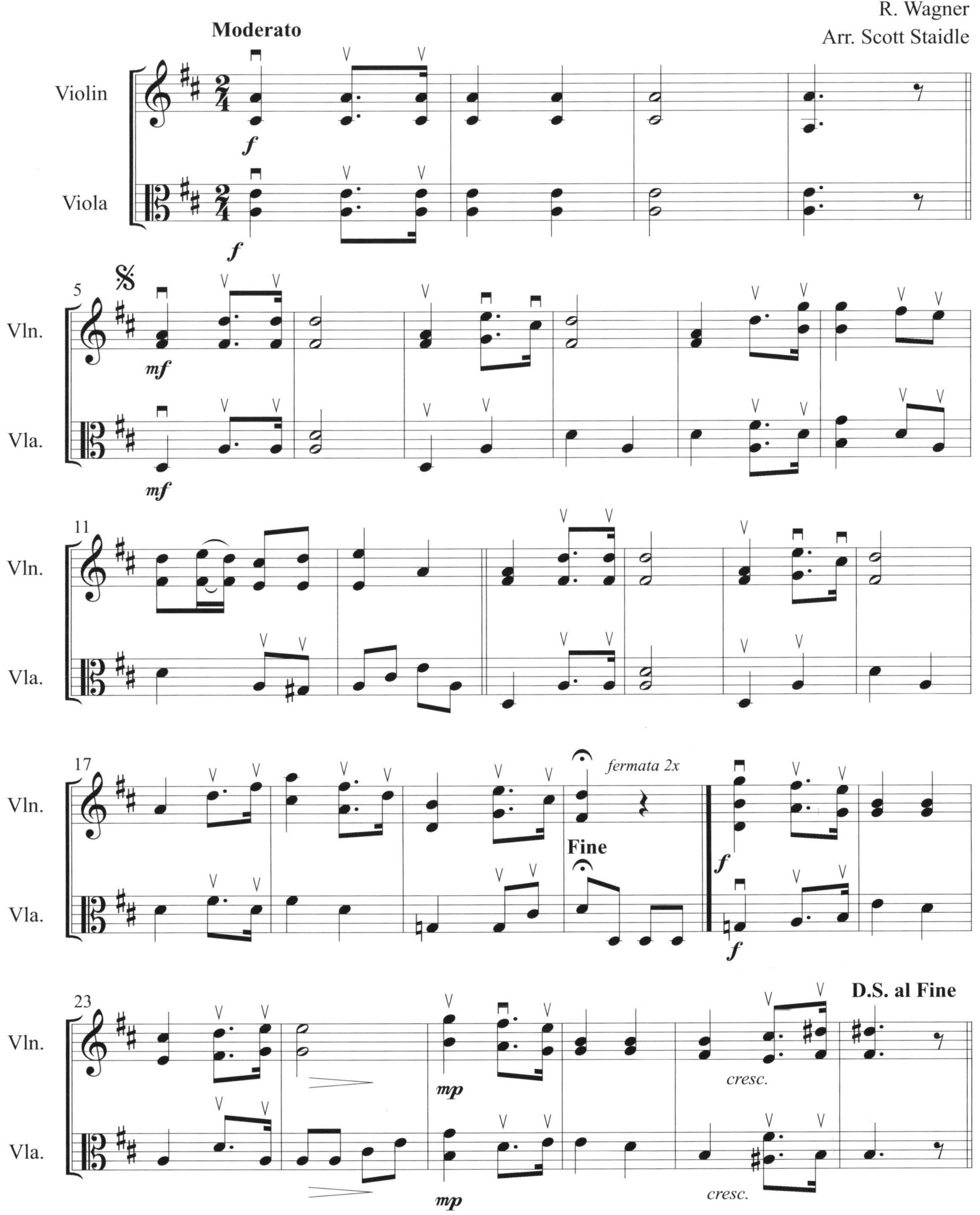

Menuetto
for Violin and Viola

Score

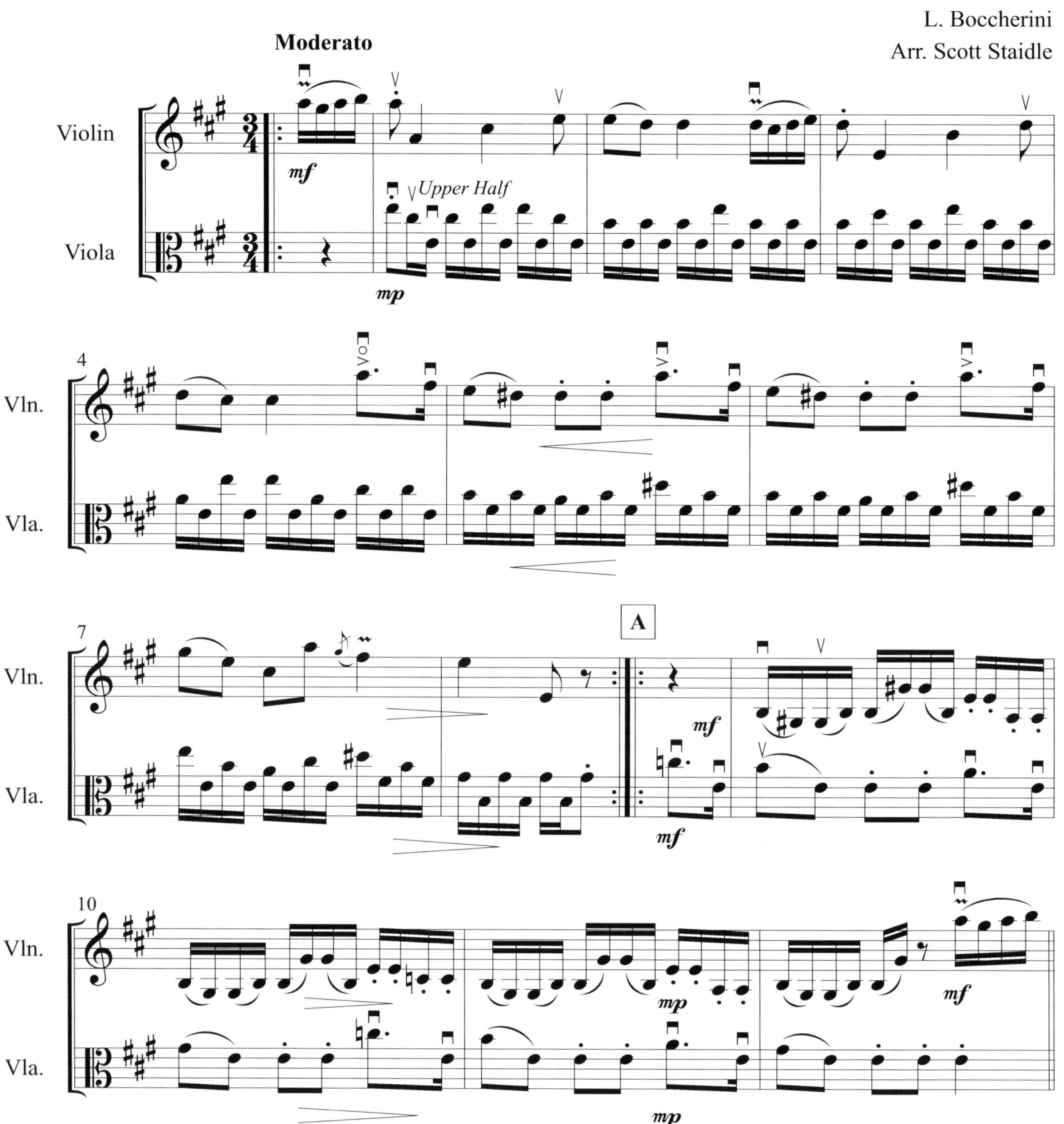

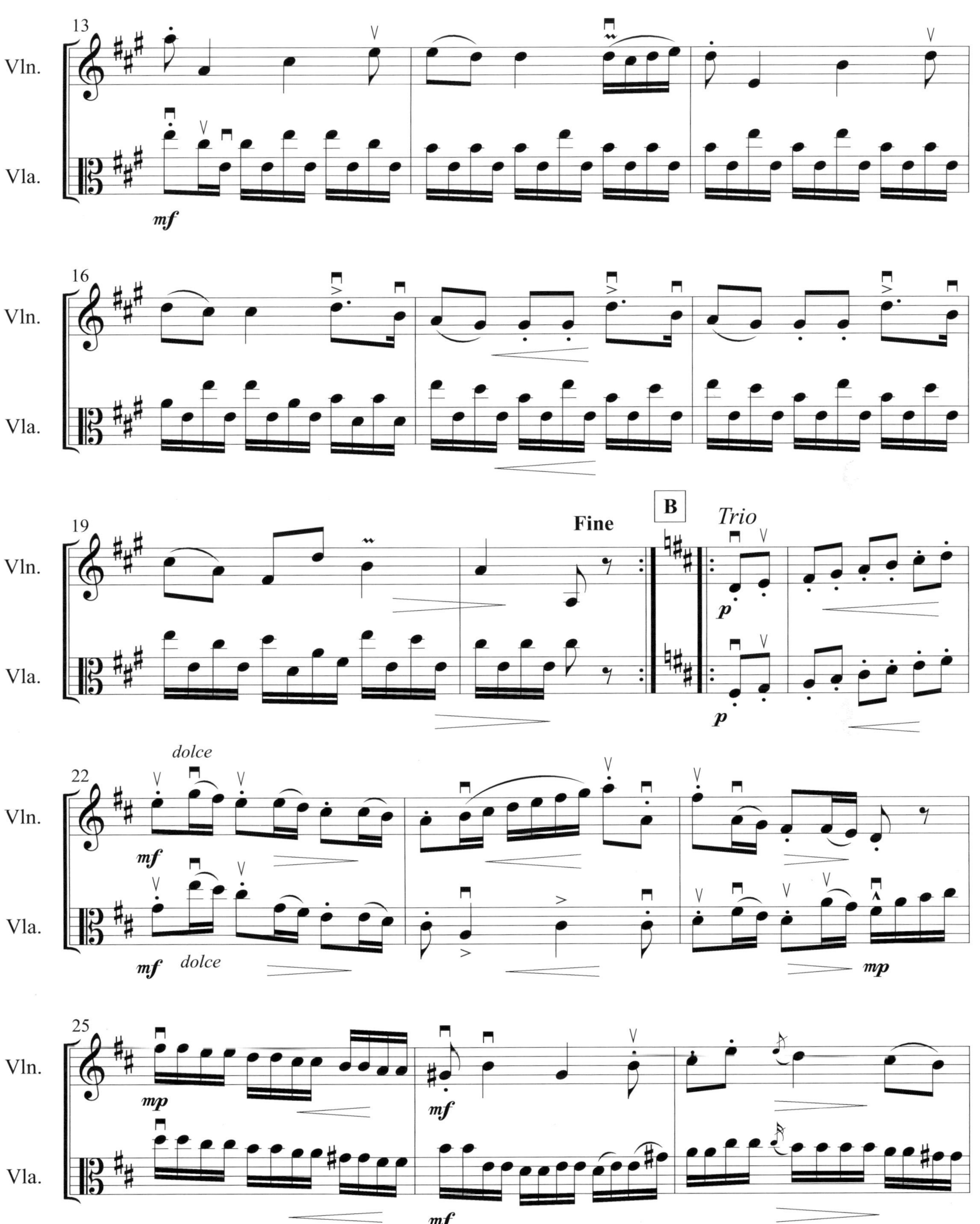
13
Vln.
Vla.
mf
16
Vln.
Vla.
19
Fine
B
Trio
Vln.
Vla.
p
p
22
dolce
Vln.
mf
Vla.
mf
dolce
mp
25
Vln.
mp
mf
Vla.
mf

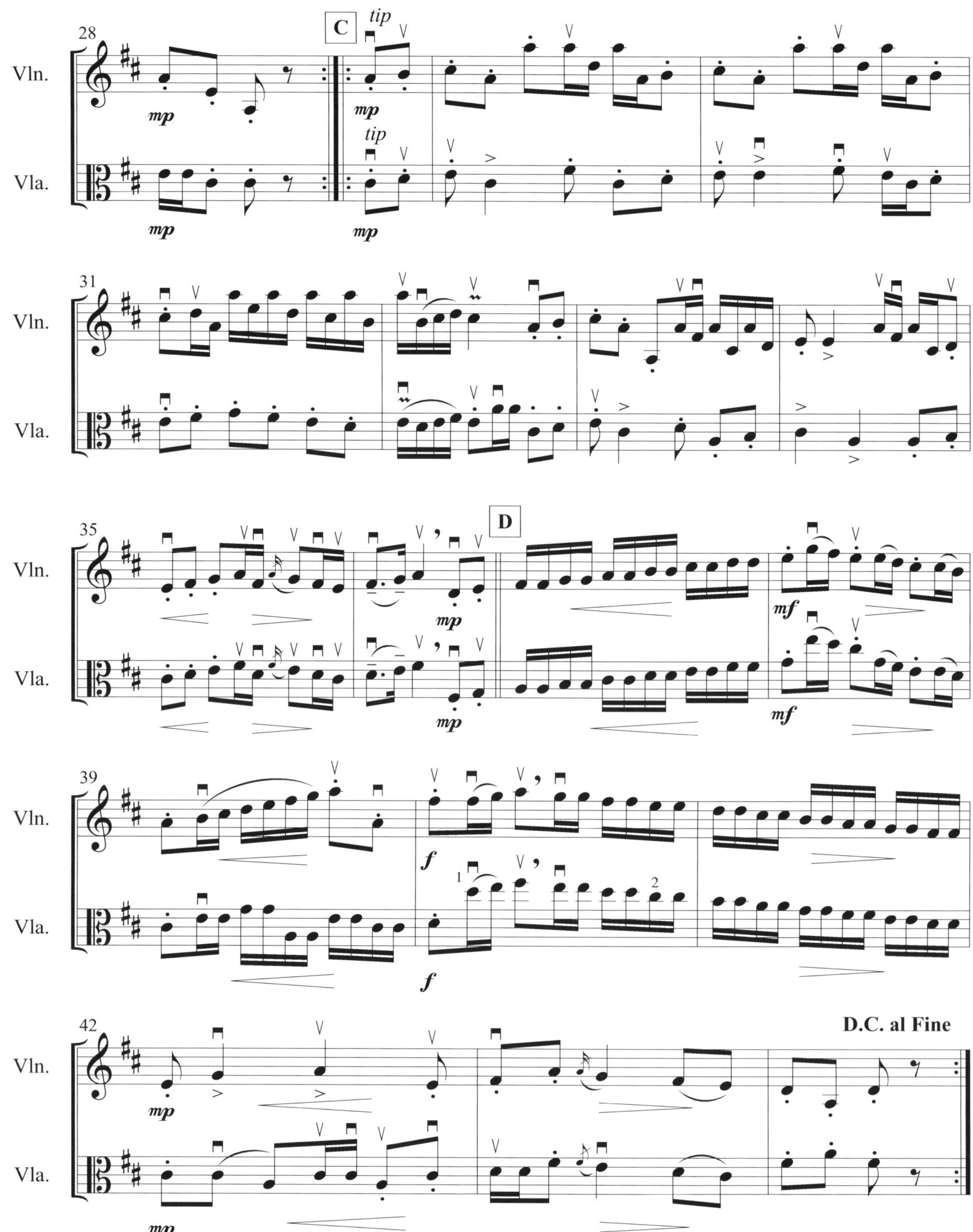

28
Vln.
Vla.
C
tip
mp
31
35
D
mf
39
f
42
D.C. al Fine

Ode to Joy
for Violin and Viola

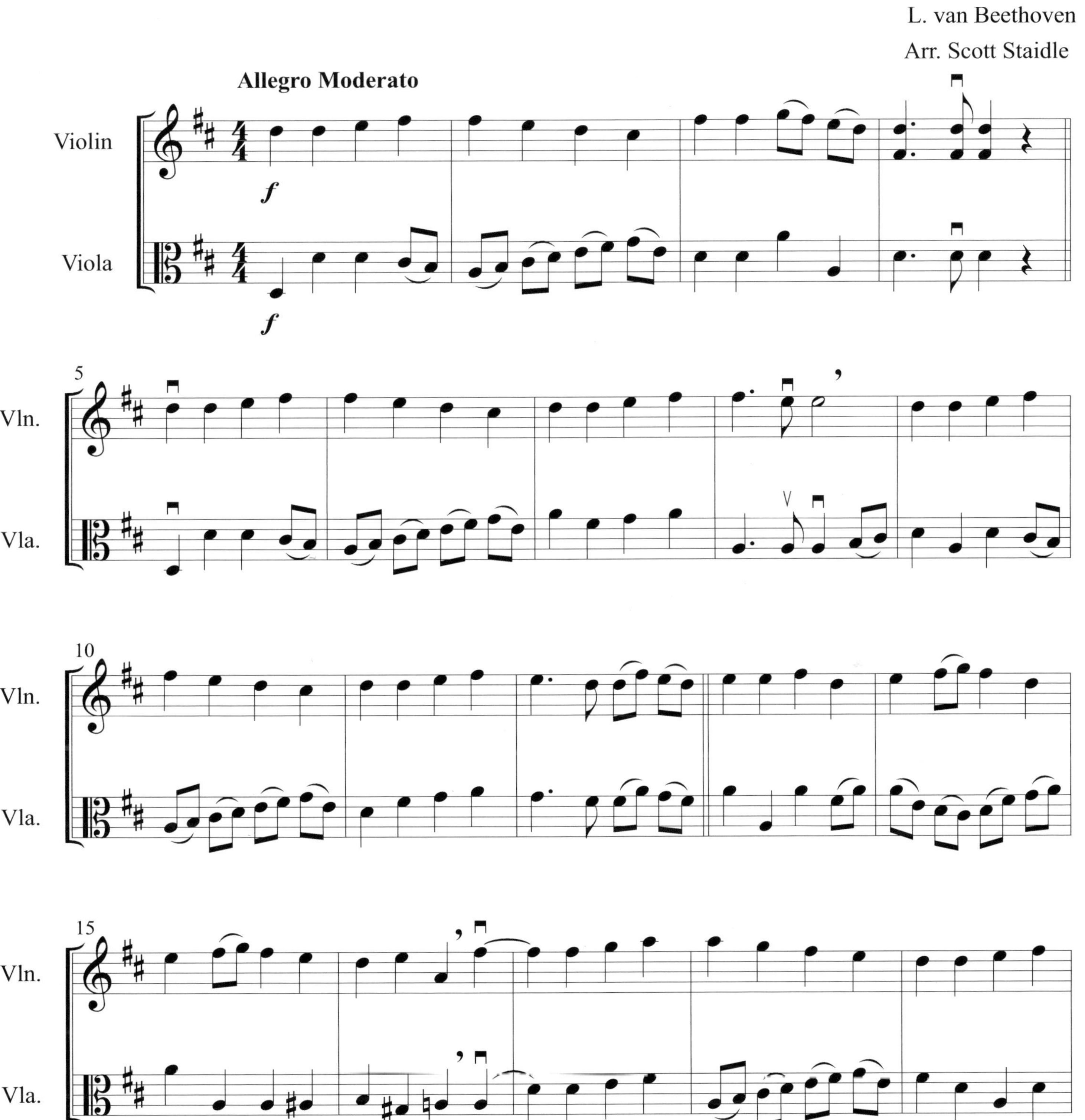

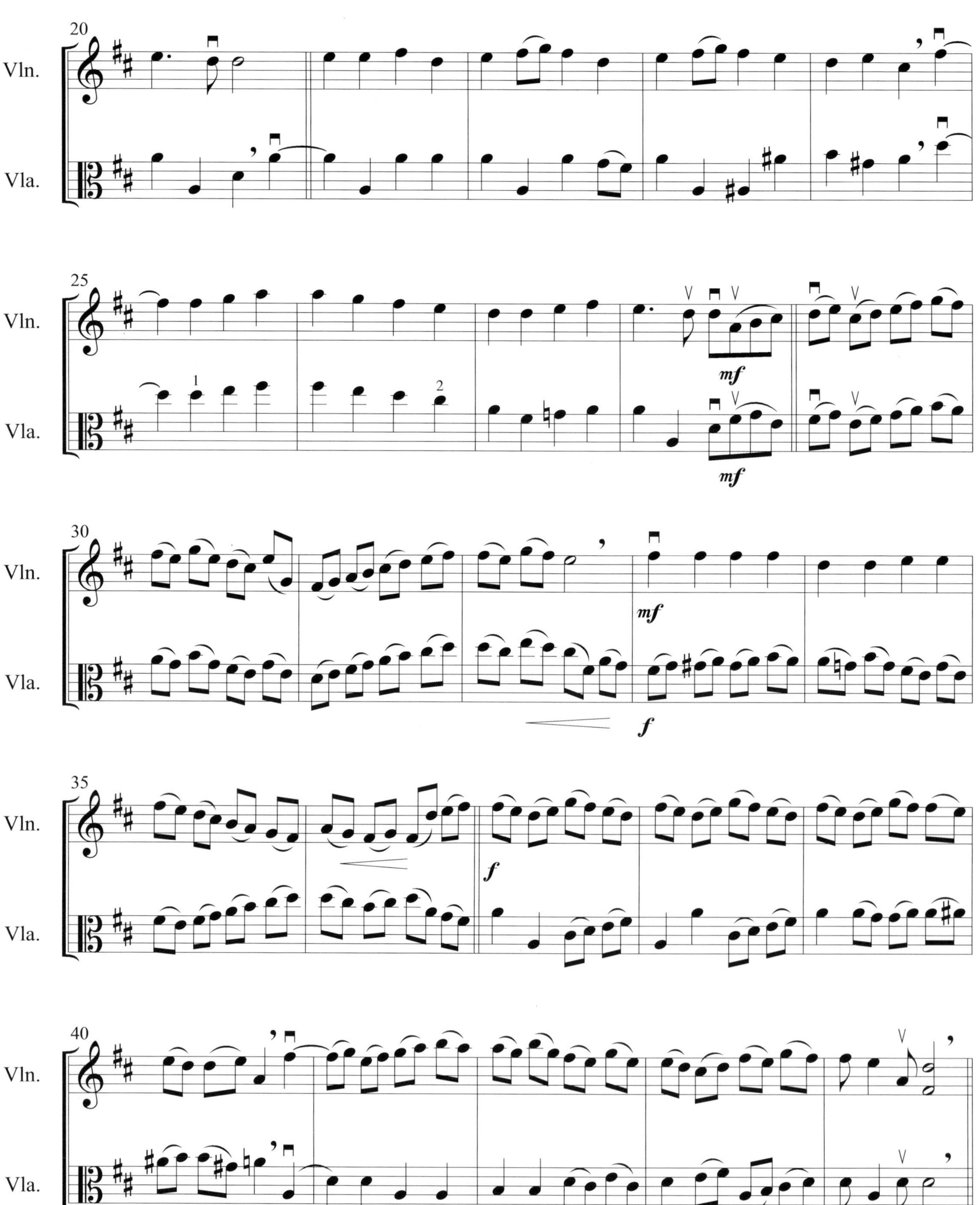
Vln.
Vla.
mf
f

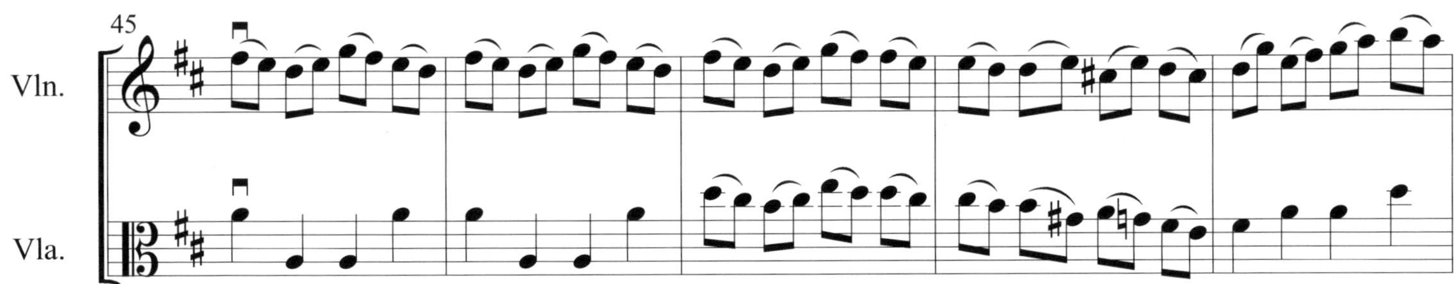
45
Vln.
Vla.

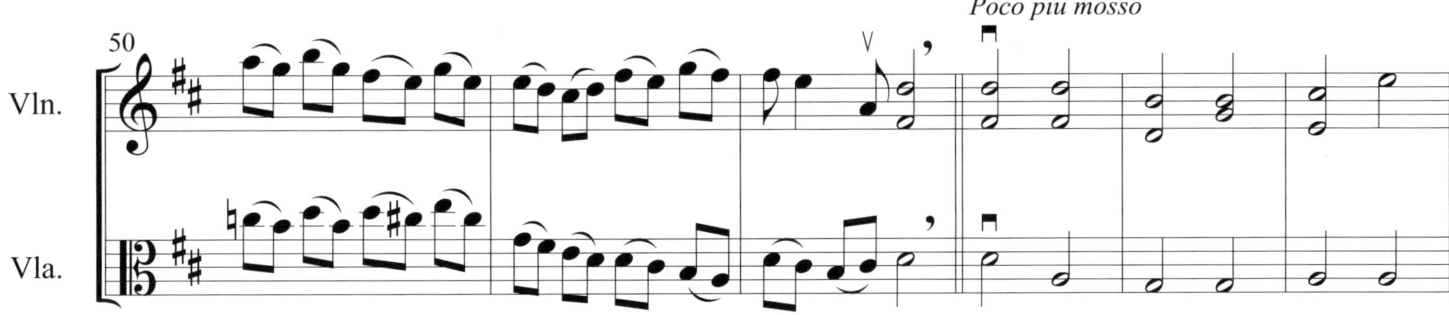
Poco piu mosso
50
Vln.
Vla.

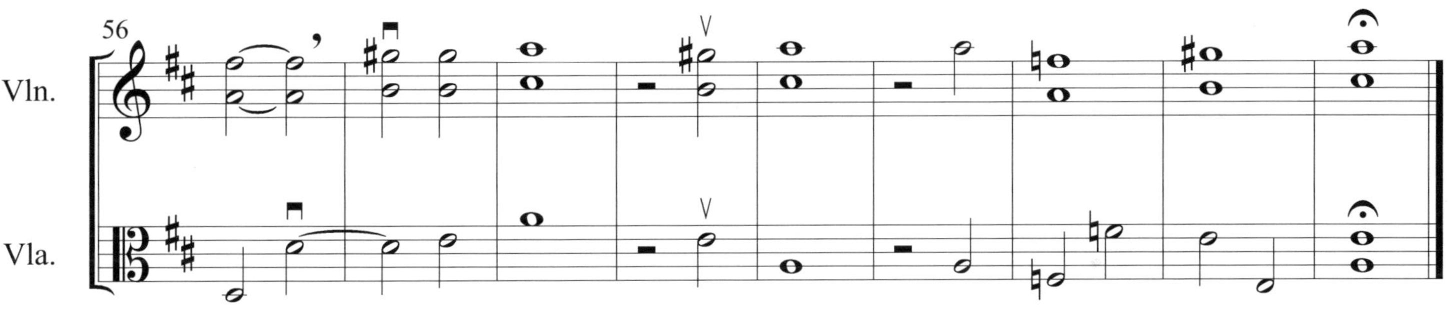
56
Vln.
Vla.

Trumpet Voluntary in "D"
for Violin and Viola

Score

H. Purcell
Arr. Scott Staidle

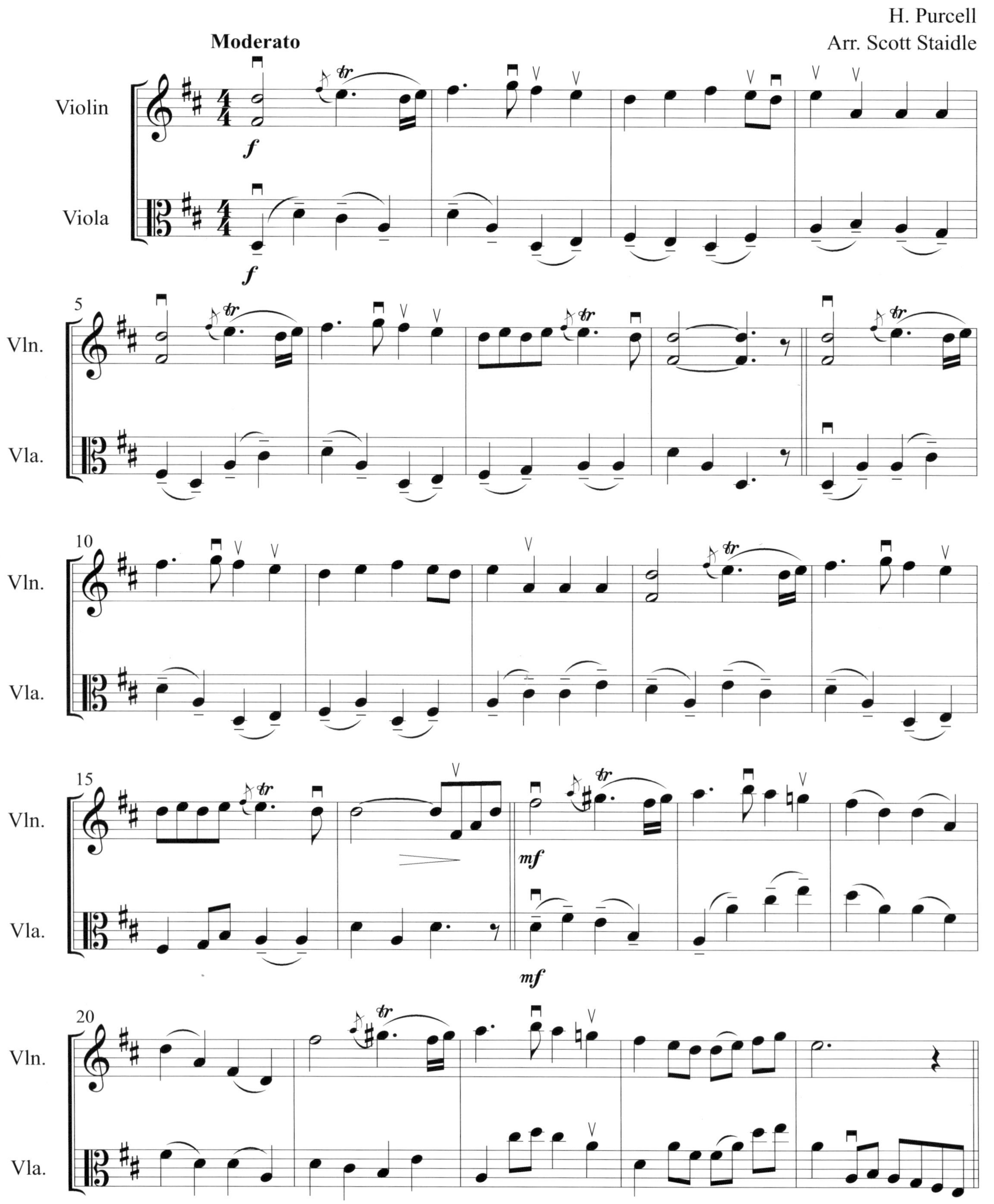

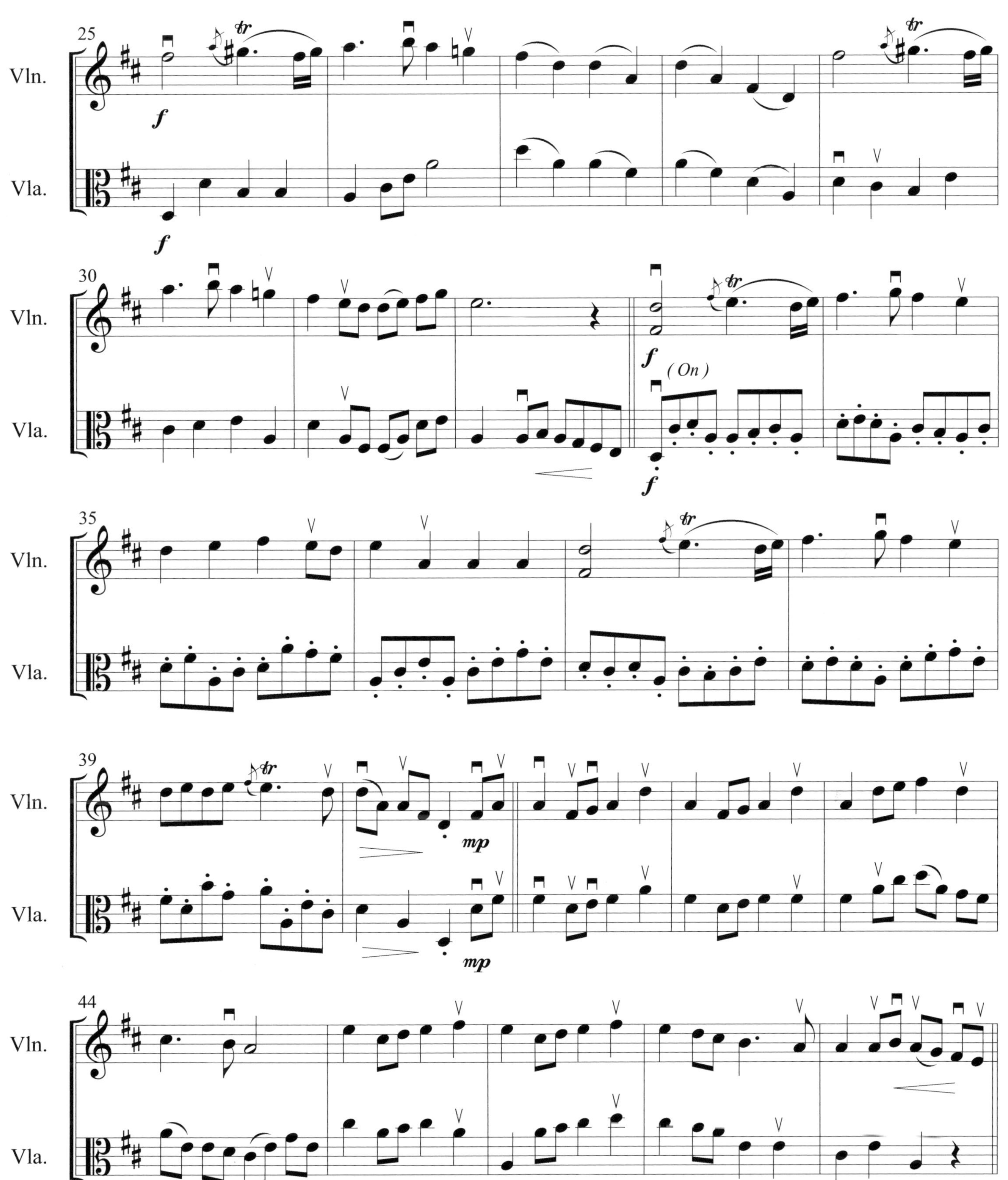
Vln.
Vla.
f
(On)
mp
tr

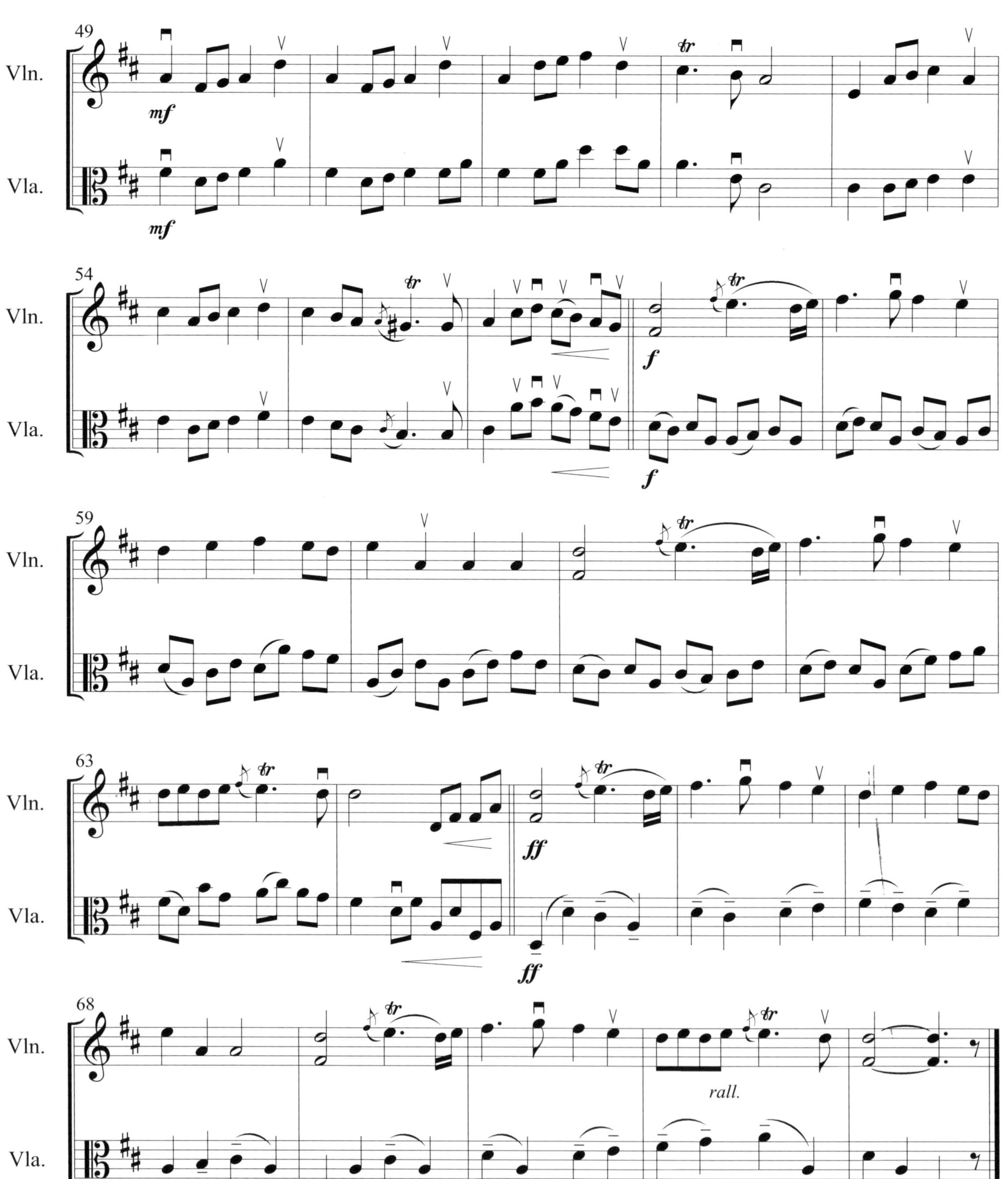
49
Vln.
Vla.
mf
mf
54
f
f
59
63
ff
ff
68
rall.

Wedding March
for Violin and Viola

Score

F. Mendelssohn
Arr. Scott Staidle

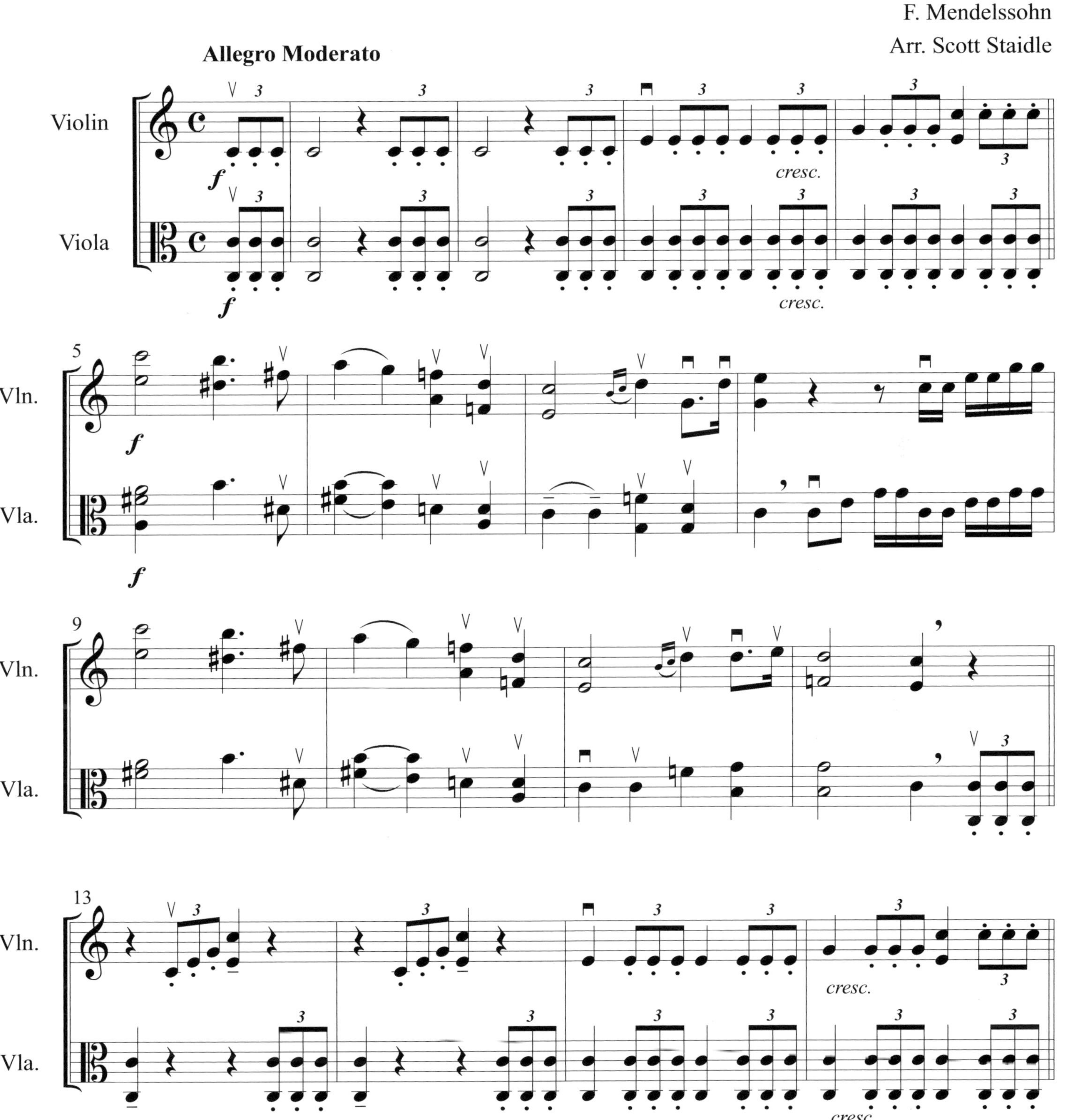

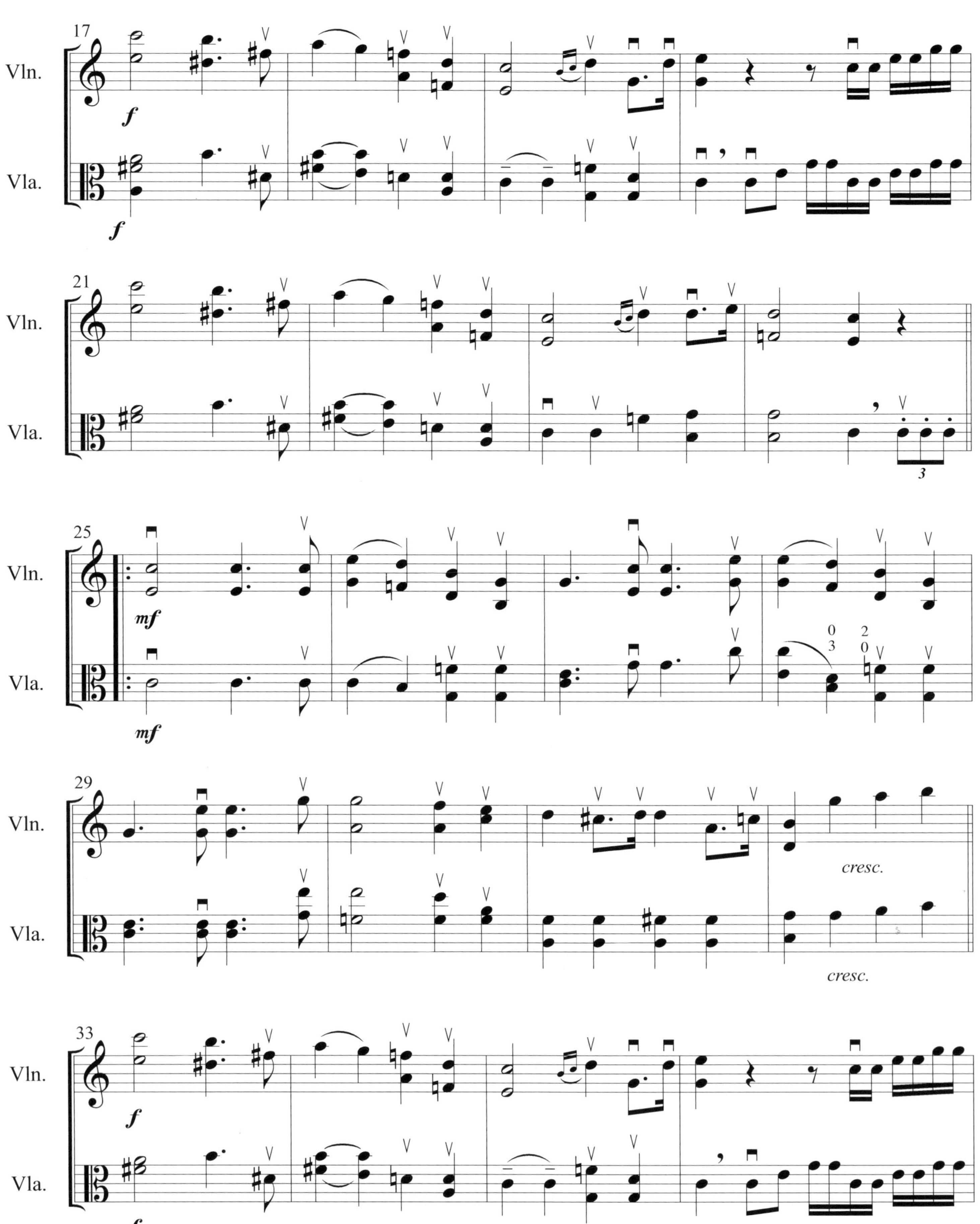

17
Vln.
Vla.
21
Vln.
Vla.
3
25
Vln.
Vla.
mf
mf
29
Vln.
Vla.
cresc.
cresc.
33
Vln.
Vla.

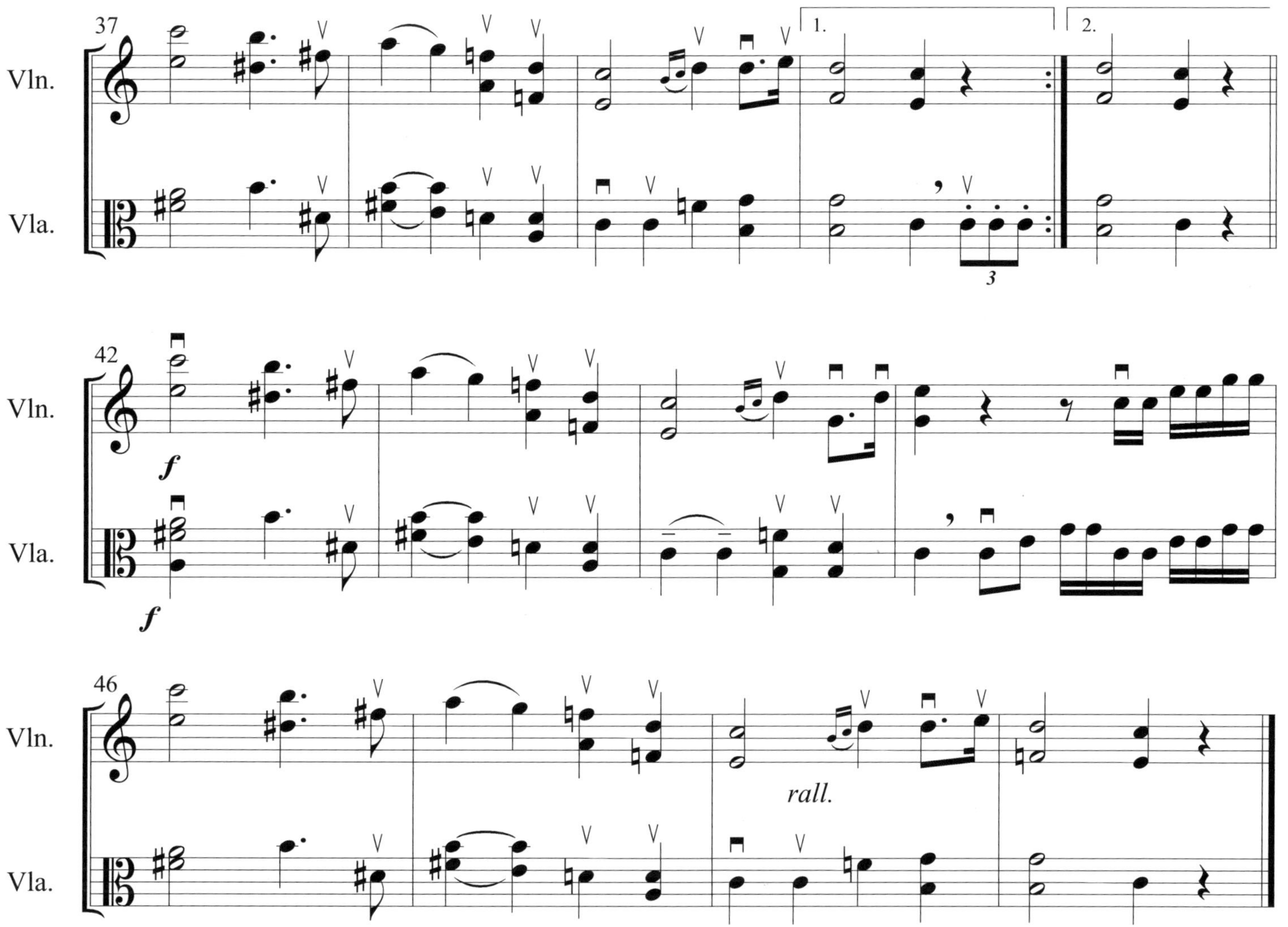
37
Vln.
Vla.
1.
2.
42
46
rall.

Rondeau
for Violin and Viola

Score

J. Mouret
Arr. Scott Staidle

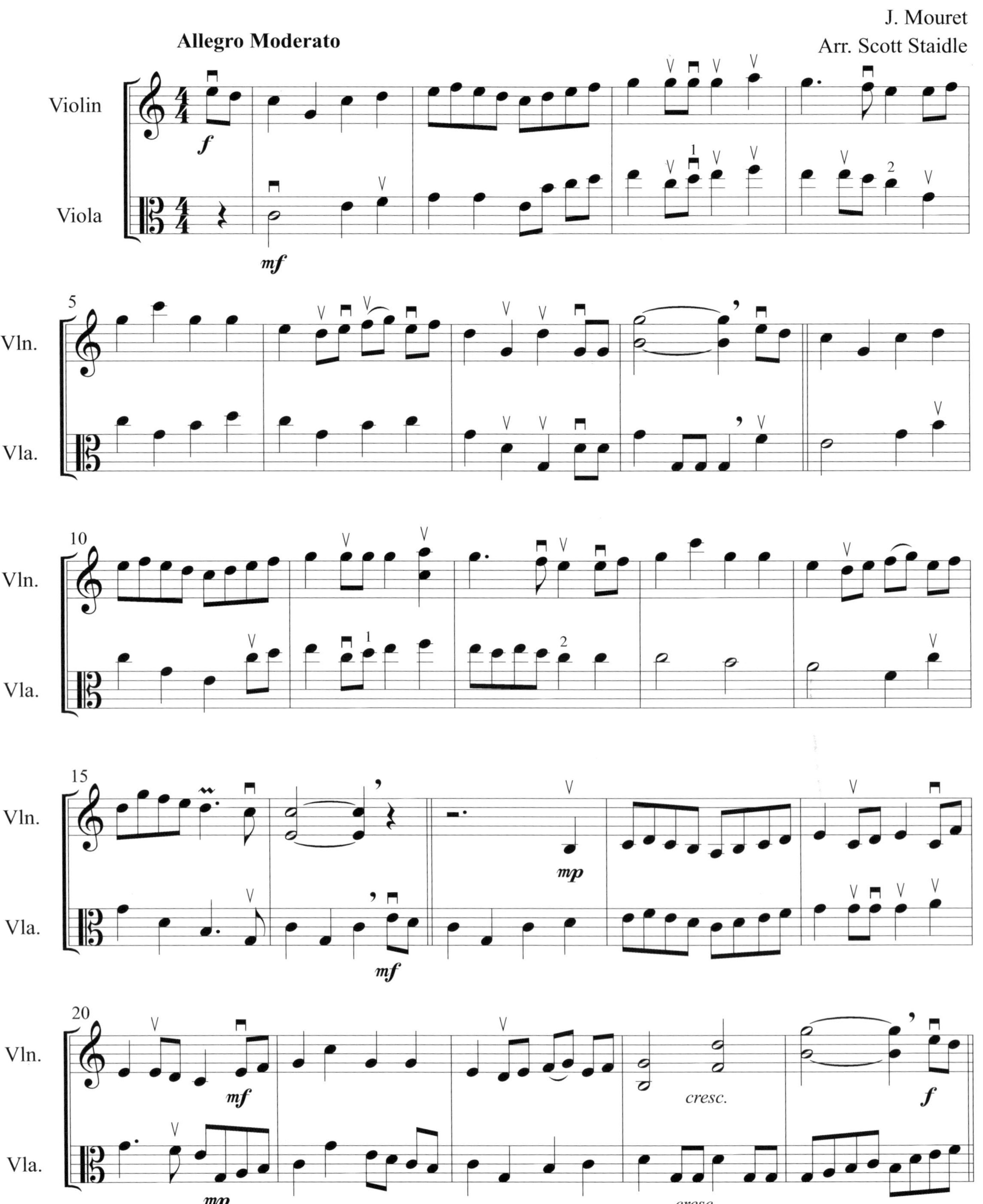

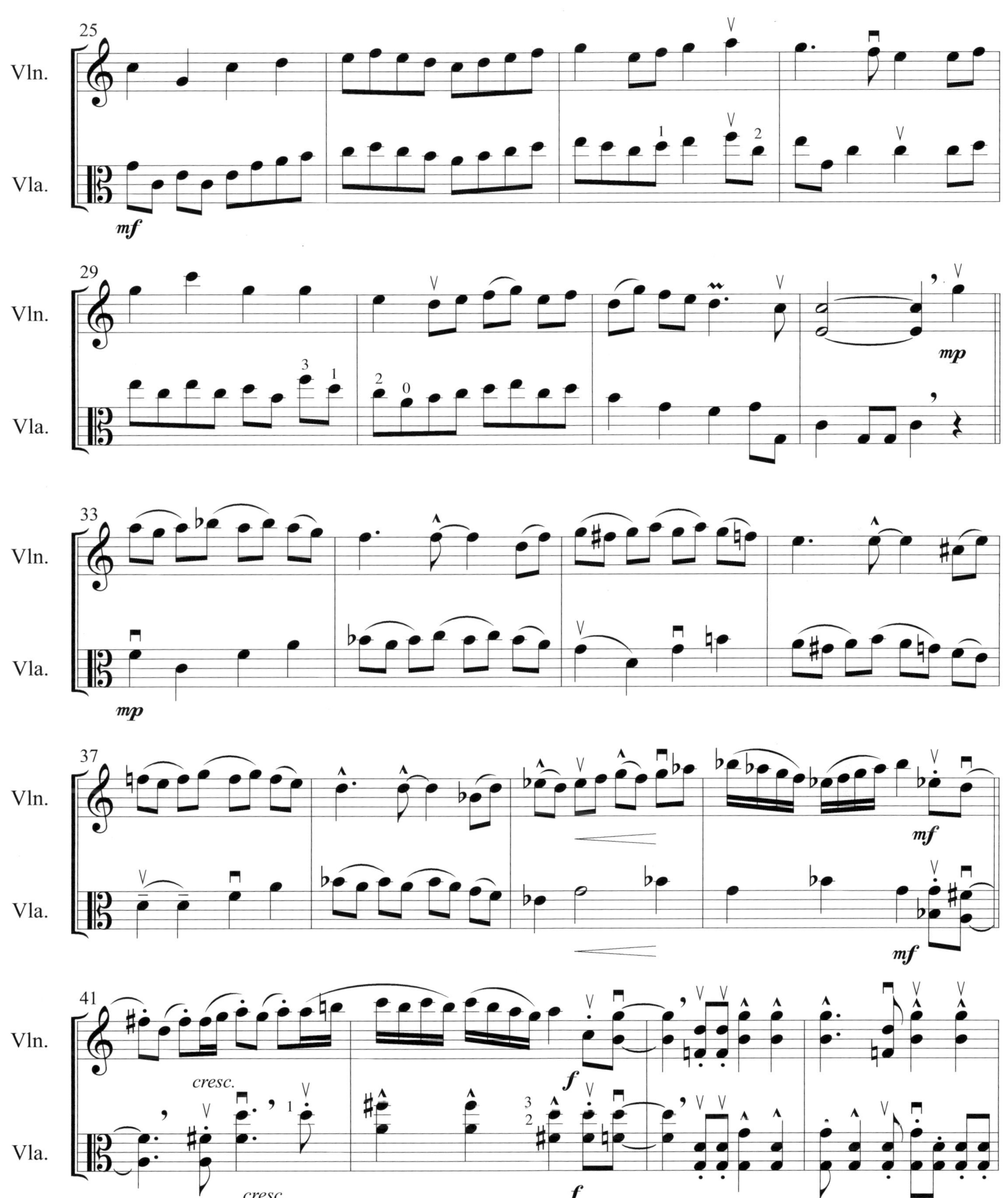
25
Vln.
Vla.
mf
29
Vln.
Vla.
mp
33
Vln.
Vla.
mp
37
Vln.
Vla.
mf
mf
41
Vln.
Vla.
cresc.
f
cresc.
f

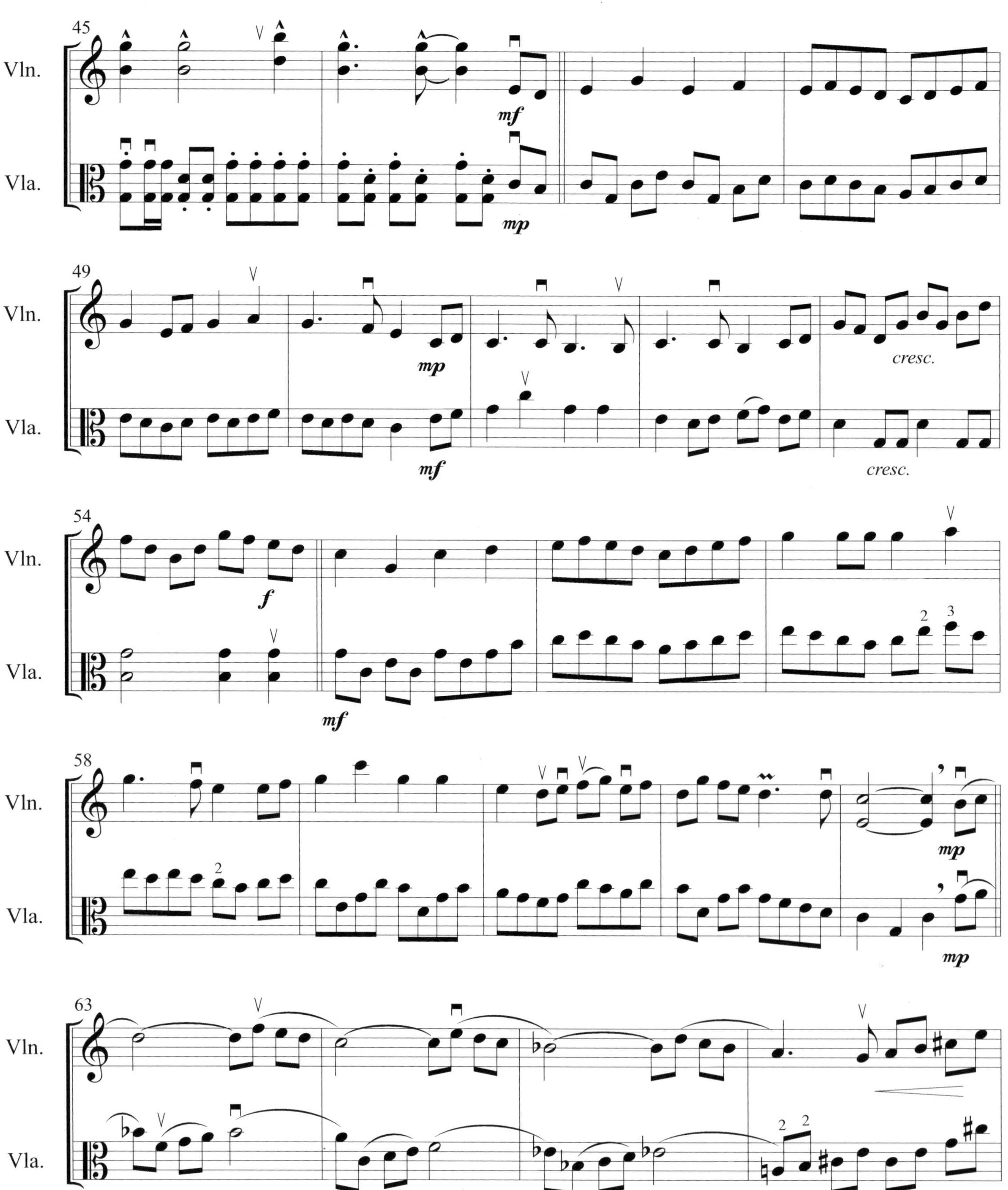
45
Vln.
Vla.
mf
mp
49
mp
mf
cresc.
cresc.
54
f
mf
58
mp
mp
63

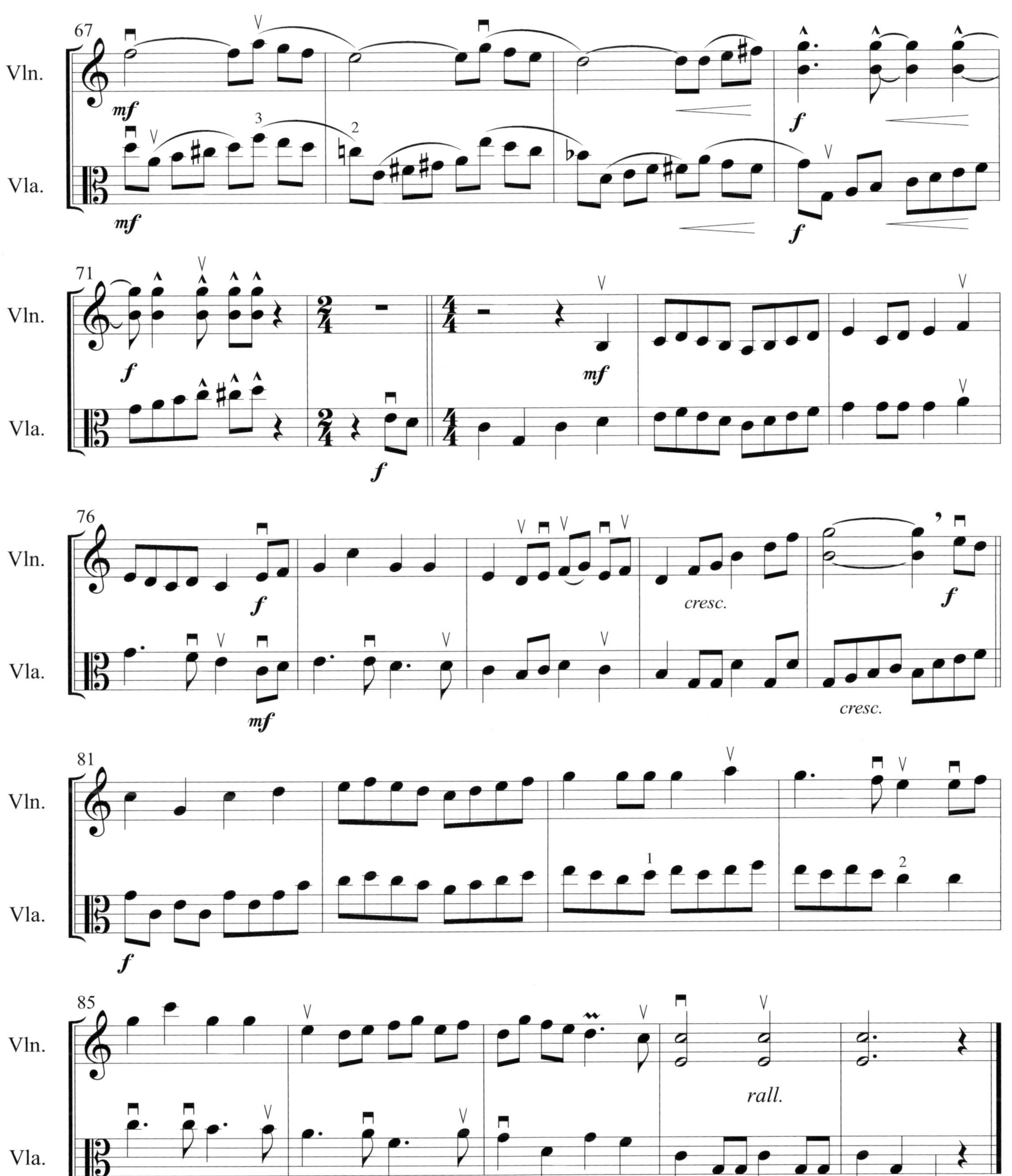

67
Vln.
Vla.
mf
3
2
f
71
2
4
mf
76
cresc.
81
1
2
85
rall.

Serenade
for Violin and Viola

Score

J. Haydn
Arr. Scott Staidle

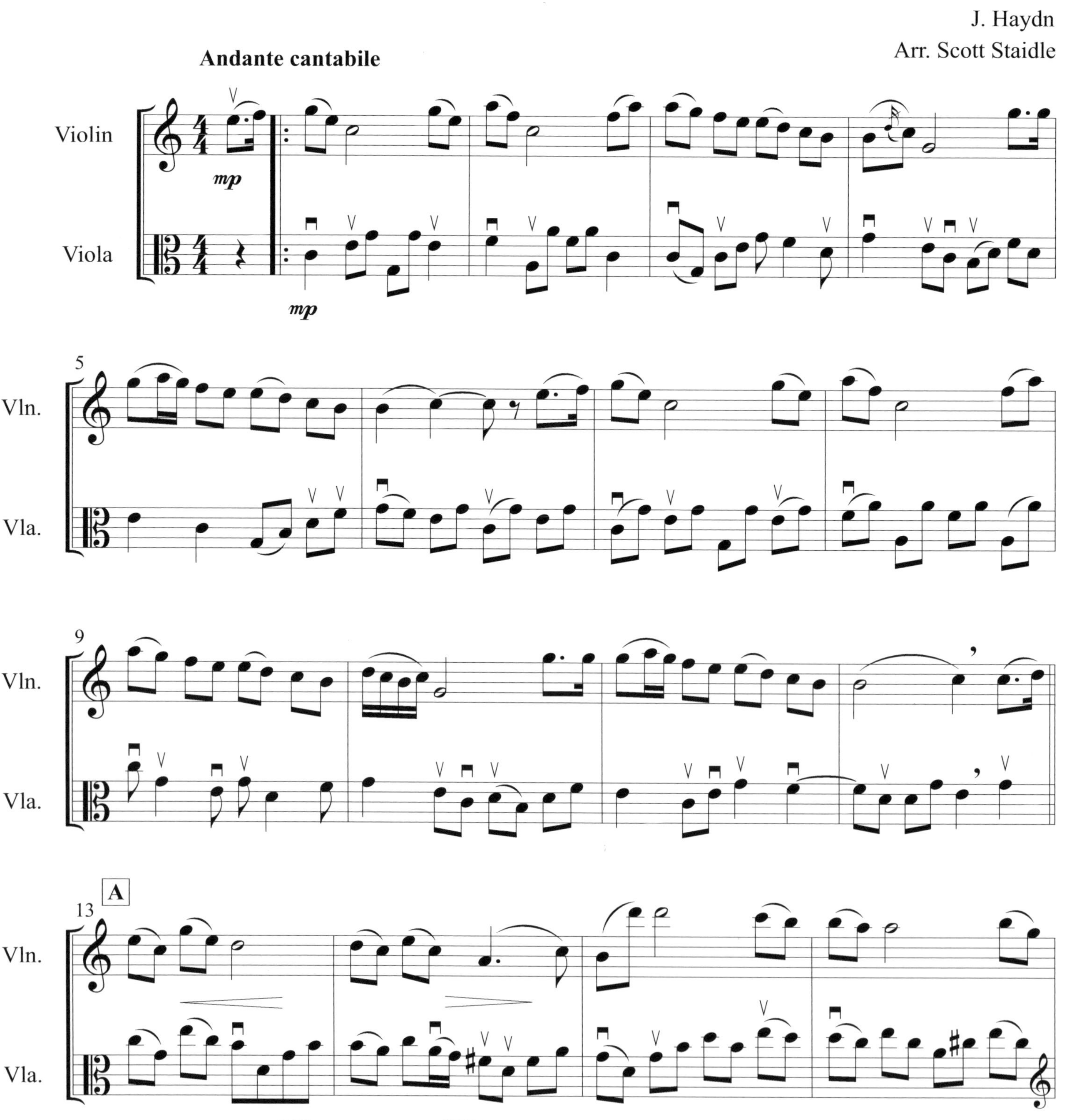

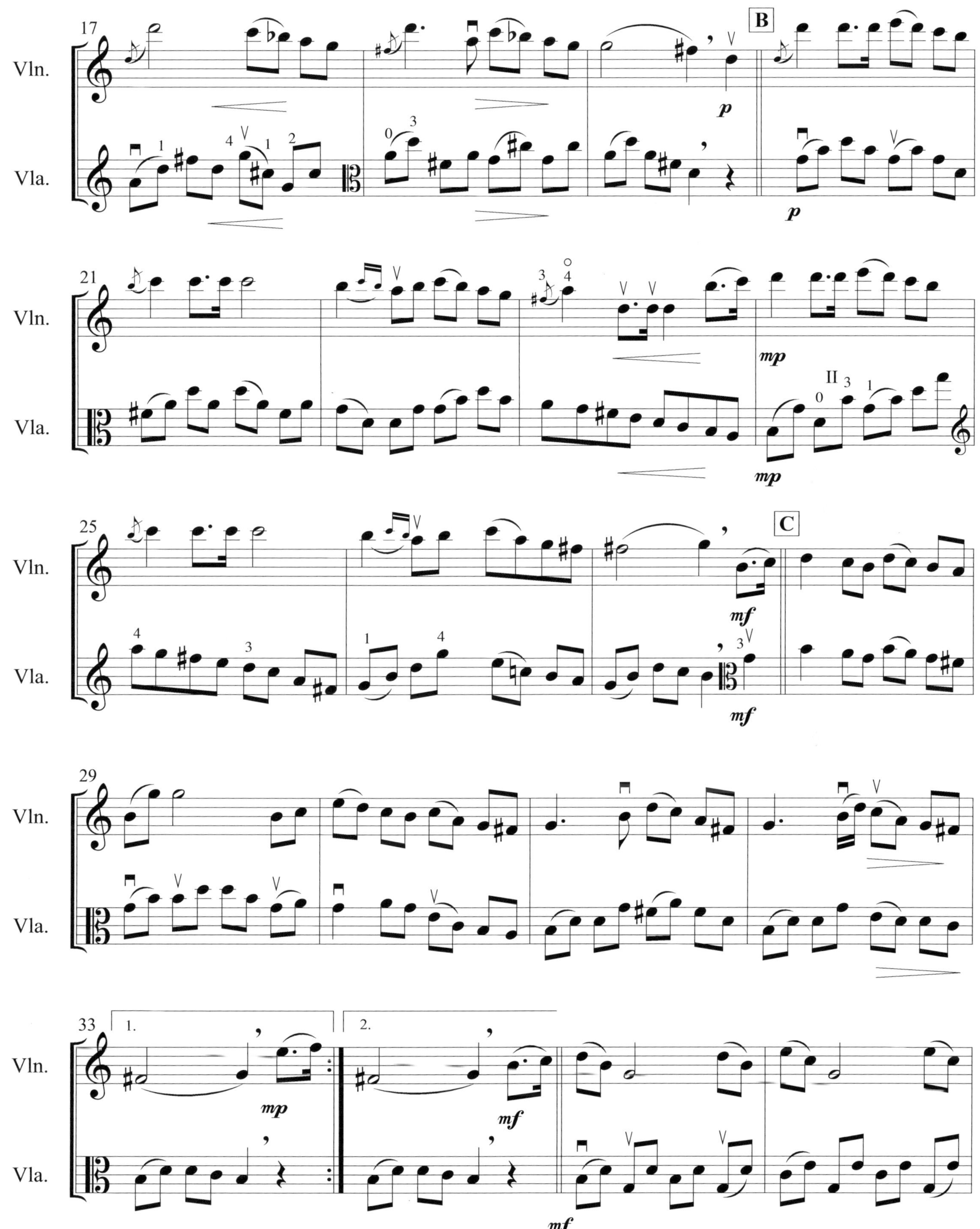

Vln.
Vla.
B
C
mp
mf
p

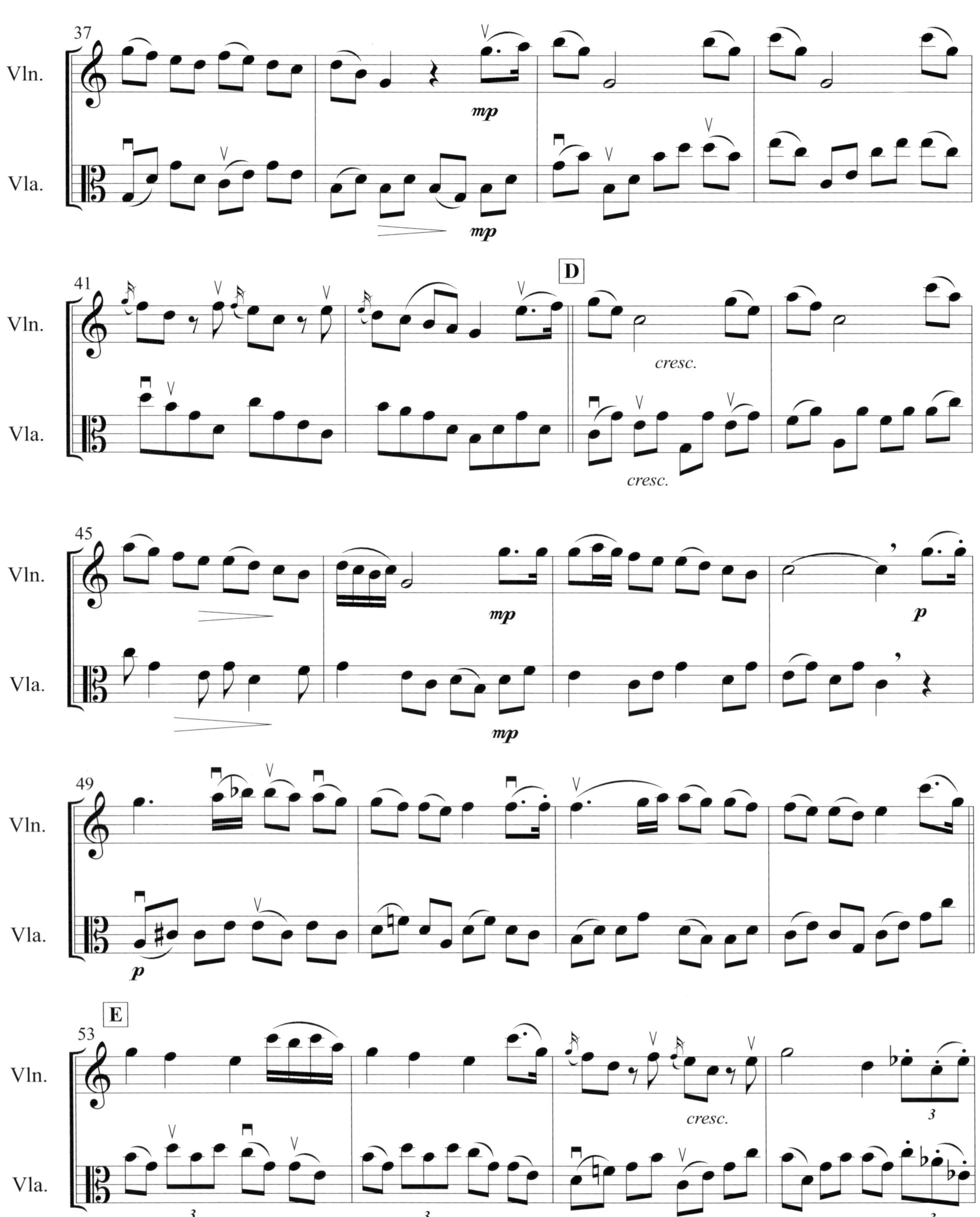

37
Vln.
Vla.
mp
mp
41
D
cresc.
cresc.
45
mp
mp
p
49
p
E
53
cresc.
cresc.
3

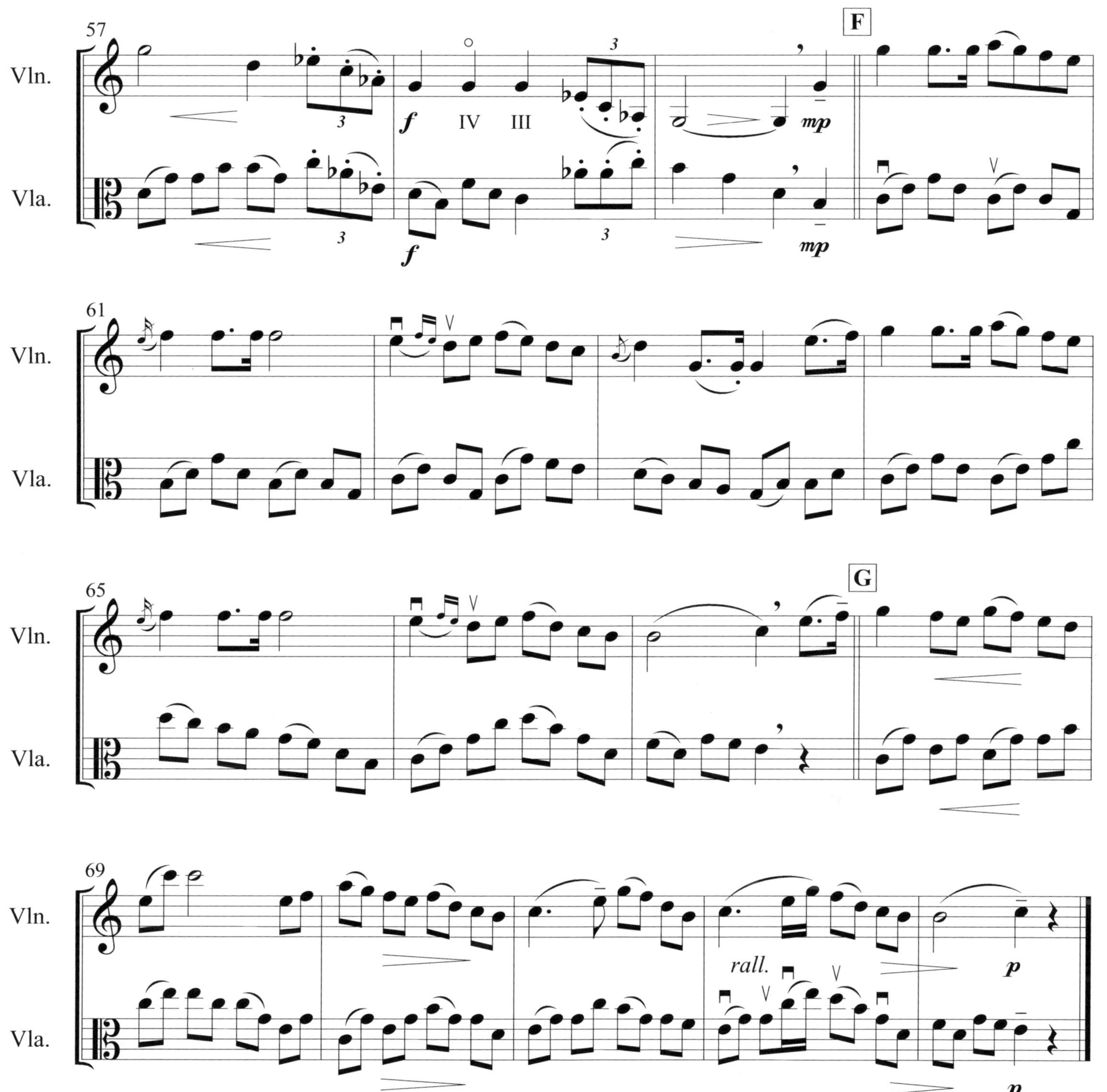

57
Vln.
Vla.
F
f
IV
III
mp
61
65
G
69
rall.
p

Water Music - Hornpipe
for Violin and Viola

Score

G. F. Handel
Arr. Scott Staidle

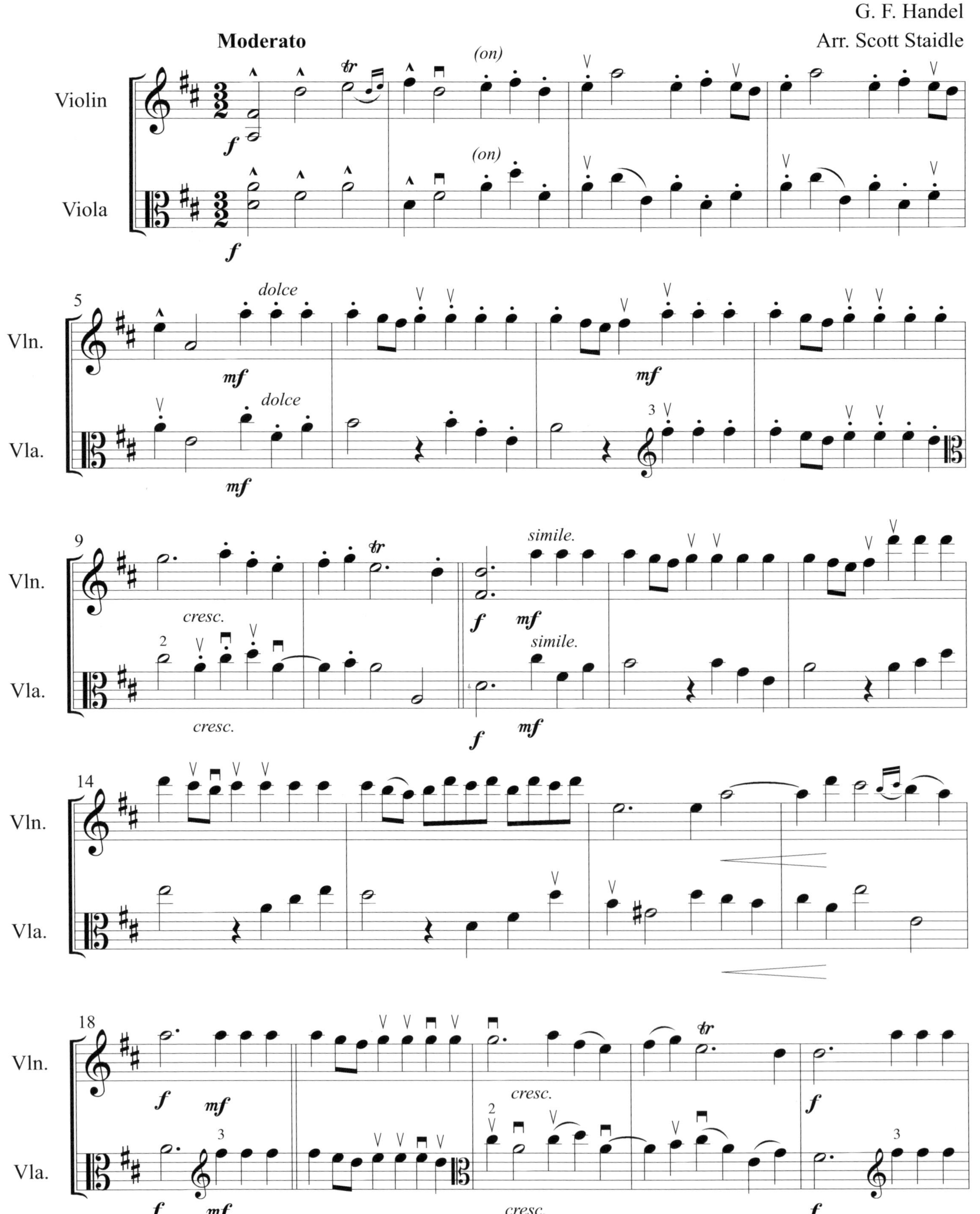

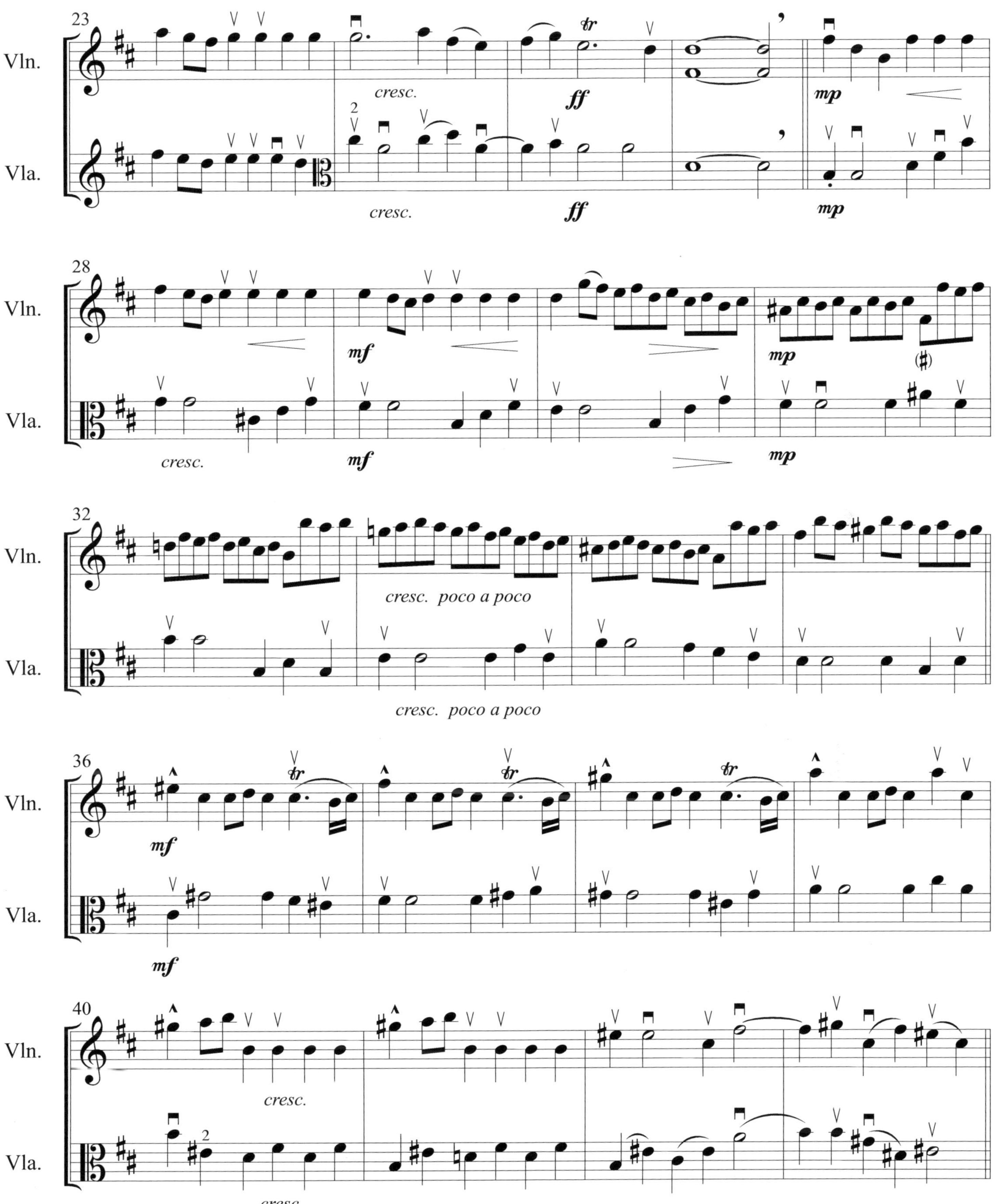
23
Vln.
Vla.
cresc.
ff
mp
cresc.
ff
mp
28
Vln.
Vla.
mf
mp
cresc.
mf
mp
32
Vln.
Vla.
cresc. poco a poco
cresc. poco a poco
36
Vln.
Vla.
mf
mf
40
Vln.
Vla.
cresc.
cresc.

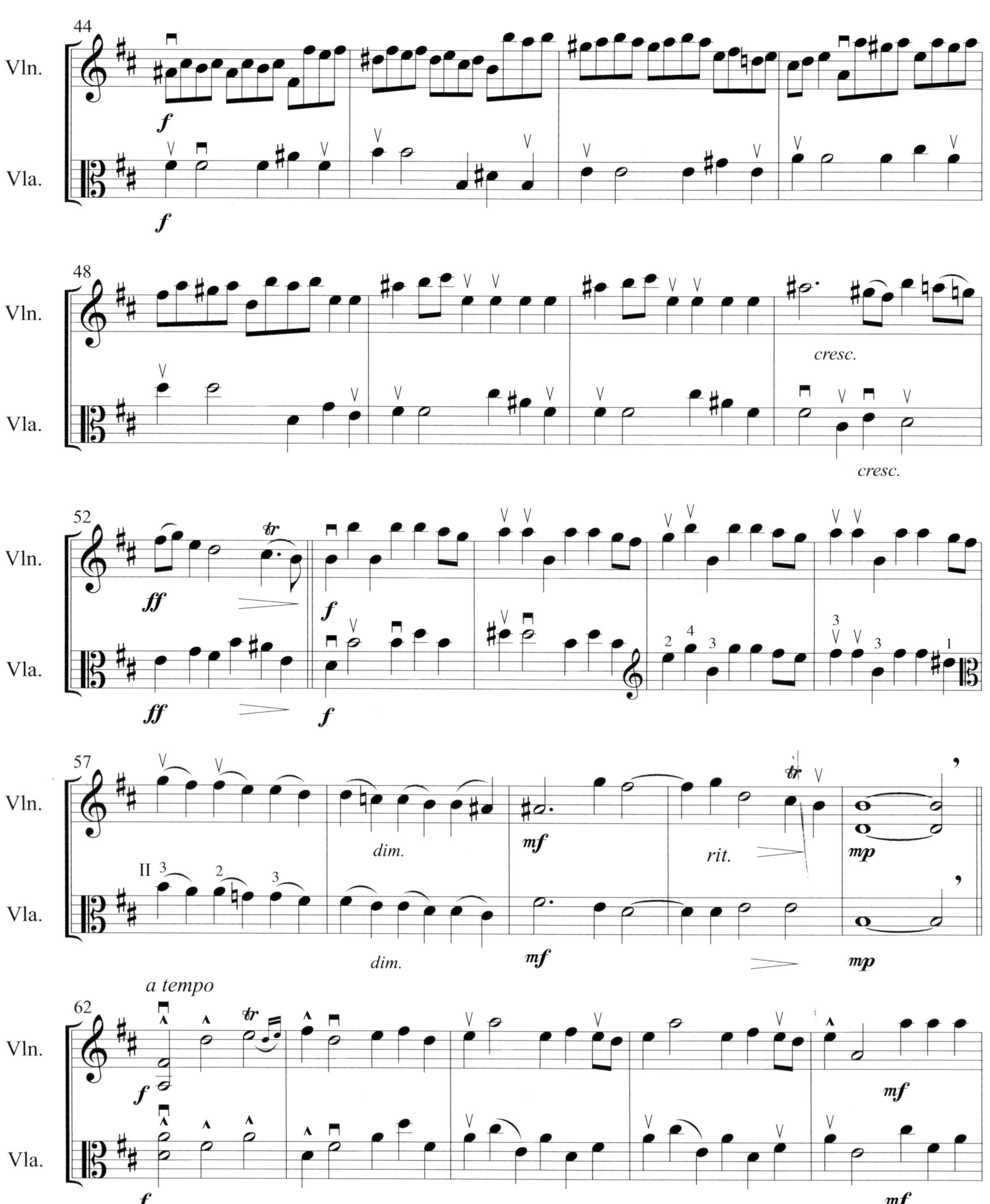
44
Vln.
Vla.
f
f
48
cresc.
cresc.
52
ff
f
ff
f
57
II
dim.
dim.
mf
mf
rit.
mp
mp
a tempo
62
f
f
mf
mf

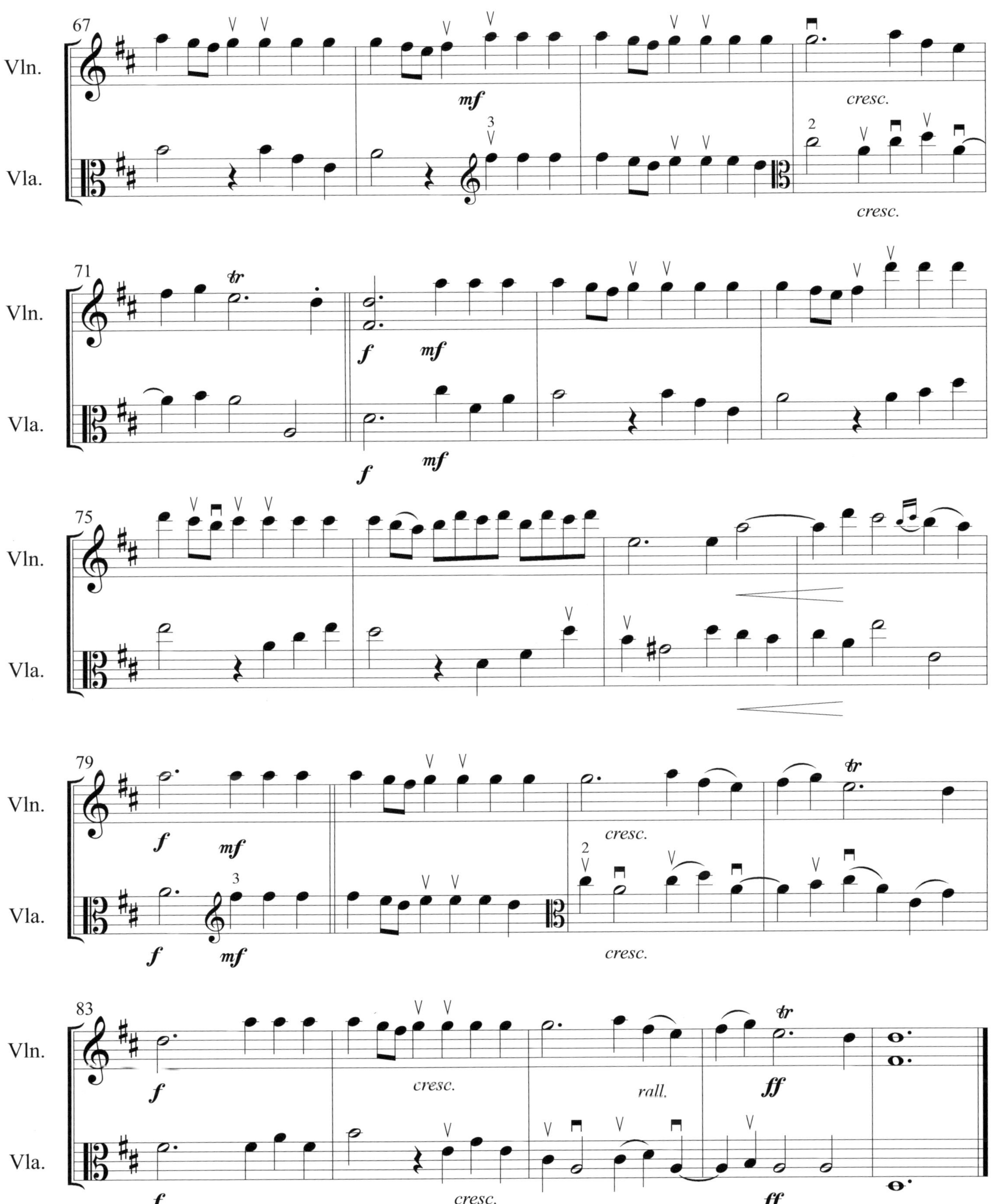
67
Vln.
Vla.
mf
cresc.
cresc.
71
tr
f
mf
f
mf
75
79
f
mf
f
mf
cresc.
tr
cresc.
83
f
cresc.
rall.
tr
ff
f
cresc.
ff

Winter - 2nd Movement from "The Four Seasons"
for Violin and Viola

Score

A. Vivaldi
Arr. Scott Staidle

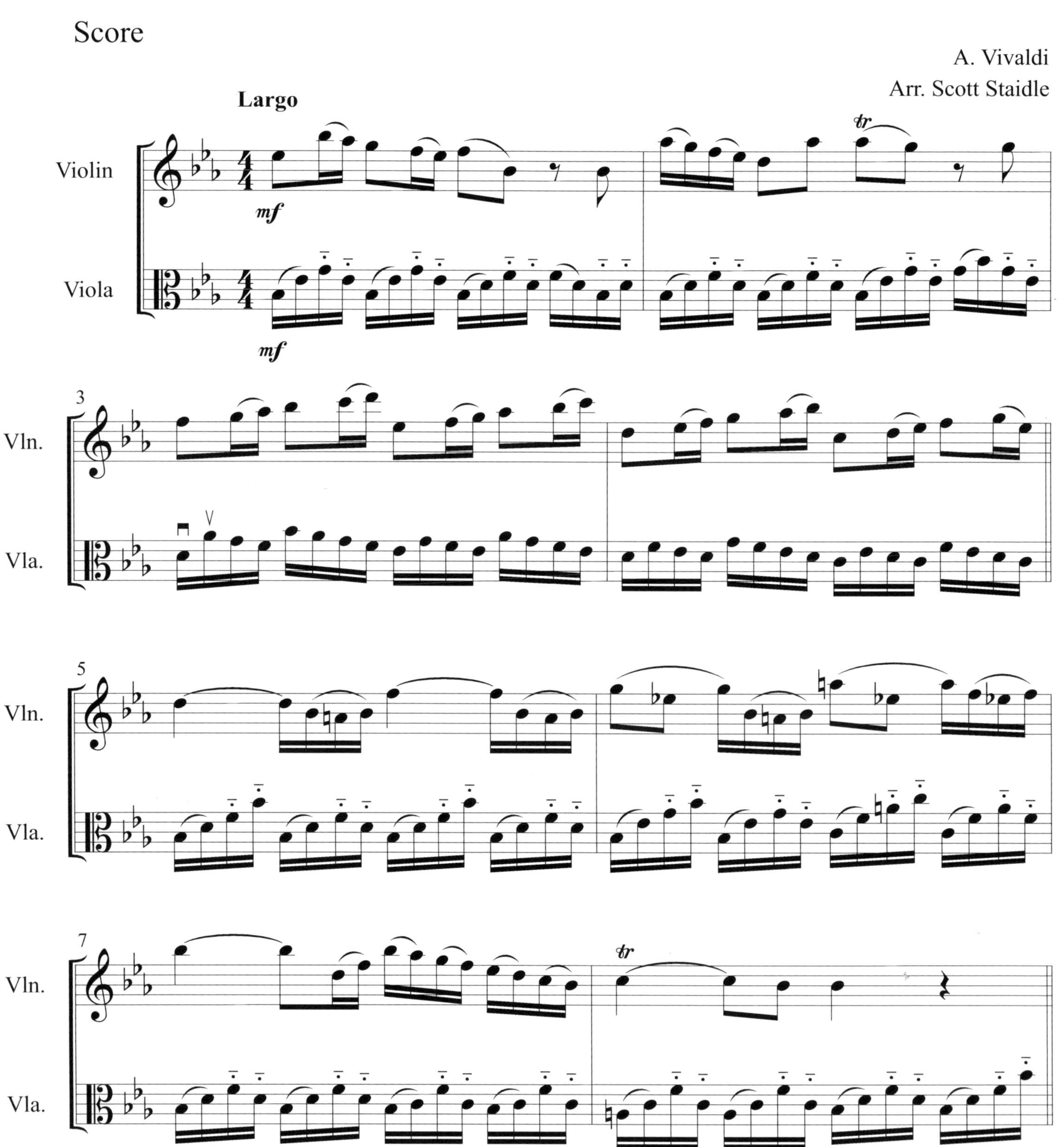

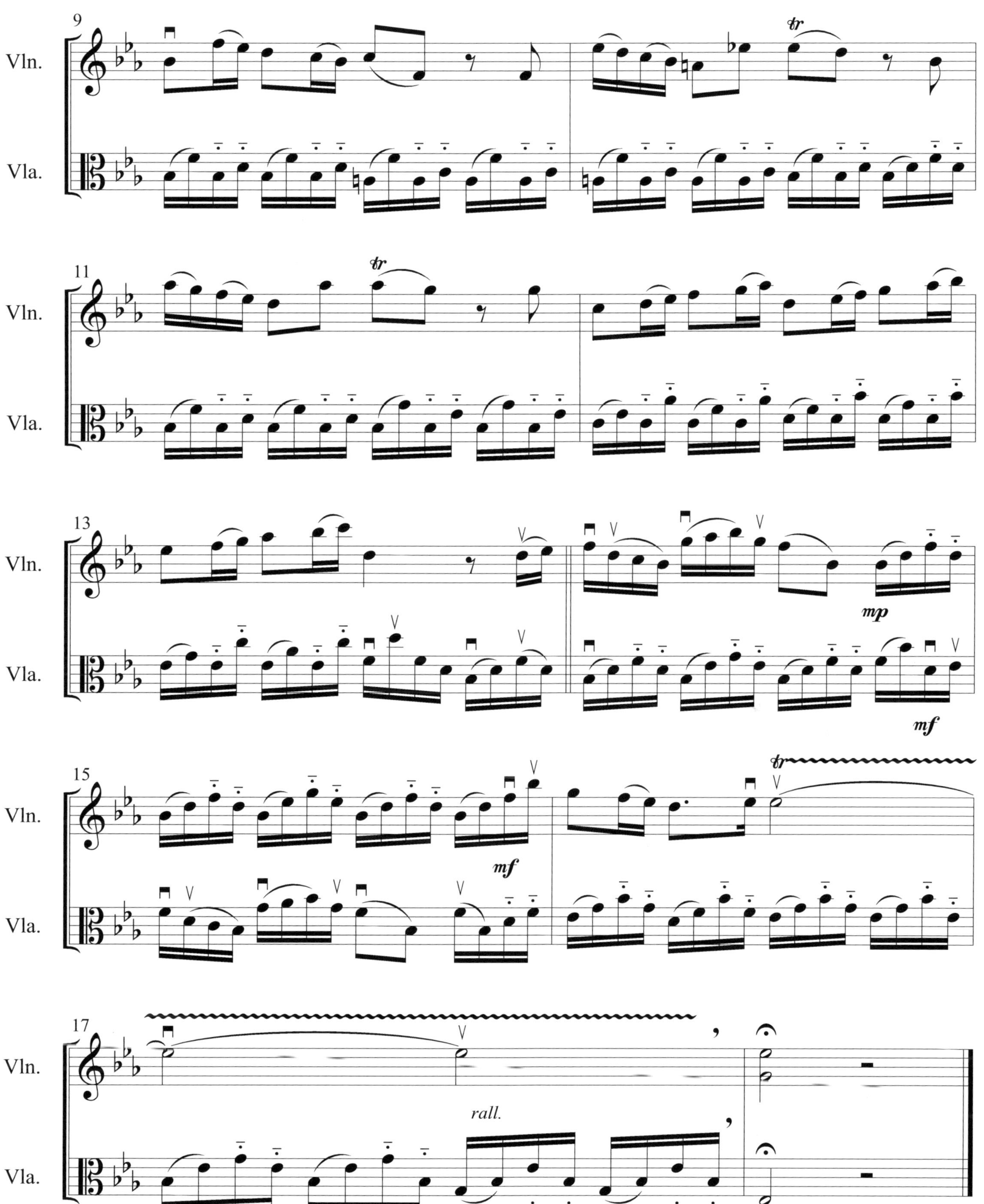

Vln.
Vla.
tr
mp
mf
rall.

Other Mel Bay Violin Books

Violin Duets and String Ensembles

American Fiddle Tunes for Solo & Ensemble: Violins 1 & 2 (C. Duncan)
Celtic Fiddle Tunes for Solo & Ensemble: Violins 1 & 2 (C. Duncan)
Christmas Music Arranged for Violin Duet (Staidle)
Christmas Strings: Violin 1 & 2 with Piano Accompaniment (Miller)
Come Fiddle with Me Volume 1 (Hay)
Come Fiddle with Me Volume 2 (Hay)
Eastern European Music for Violin Duet (Harbar)
Easy Duets for Violin (Puscoiu)
Easy Violin Duets in First Position (Isaac)
Fiddling Classics for Solo & Ensemble: Violins 1 & 2 (C. Duncan)
J. S. Bach: Duets for Two Violins (Spencer/Engle)
Jazz Duets: Violin Edition (Biondi)
Music from Around the World for Solo & Ensemble: Violins 1 & 2 (Miller)
Ragtimes for Two Violins (Brydern)
Scottish Airs and Dances for Two Violins (Witt)
Scottish Melodies for Two Violins (Witt)
Twin Fiddling (Phillips)
Violin Duet Classics Made Playable (Harbar)
Wedding Music for Two Violins (Staidle)

Violin Scales, Study and Technique

Complete Violin Scale Dictionary (Isaac)
Concept and Study for the Violinist (Lobko)
Daily Scale Exercises for the Violinist (Chang)
Finger Positions for the Violin (Gilland)
Forty Studies for Violin (Chang)
Past the Print (Waller)
Pluggin In: A Guide to Gear and New Techniques for the 21st Century Violinist (Deninzon)
Practice for Performance for Violin (DeForest)
Progressive Scale Studies for Violin (Bauer)
Sensible Scales Plus! (Waller)
Speed-Reading for Violin (Bauer)
The Violin/Fiddle Manual and Encyclopedia of Techniques:
How to Do Anything on the Iment (Willis)
Warm-Ups for the Violinist (Wheeler)

Other Mel Bay Violin Books

100 Christmas Carols and Hymns for Violin and Guitar (C. Duncan)
100 Gospel Songs and Hymns for Violin and Guitar (C. Duncan)
100 Hymns for Violin and Guitar (W. Bay/C. Duncan)
Christmas Melodies for Violin Solo (C. Duncan)
Christmas Solos for Beginning Violin (C. Duncan)
Complete Book of Wedding Music for Flute or Violin (Mickelson)
Gospel Violin (Guest)
Hymn Favorites for Violin (Abell)
Hymn Tunes for Unaccompanied Violin (Carlson)
Hymns for Violin Made Easy (Clarke)
Old English Hymns for Violin Solo (Cummings)
Sacred Hymns for Violin (Isaac)
Sacred Violin Solos (Isaac)
Sacred Melodies for Violin Solo (C. Duncan)
Violin Solos on Early American Hymns Tunes (C. Duncan)
Wedding Music for Solo Violin (Curatolo)
Easy Klezmer Tunes (Phillips)
French Tangos for Violin (Norgaard)
Gypsy Violin (Harbar)
Gypsy Violin Classics (Harbar)
Gypsy Violin Basics (Harbar)
Klezmer Collection: C Instruments (Phillips)
Lover's Waltz: Violin Solo or Duet with Piano Accompaniment (J. Ungar)
Easy Clasics for Violin with Piano Accompaniment (Spitzer)
Easy Solos for Violin (Bluestone)
My Very Best Christmas/Violin (Khanagov)
Solo Pieces for the Beginning Violinist (Duncan)
Solo Pieces for the Intermediate Violinist (Duncan)
Jazz Violin Solos (Abell)
Joe Venuti: Never Before...Never Again
Stephane Grappelli Gypsy Jazz Violin (Kliphuis)
Swingin' Jazz Fiddle Solos (Weinstein)

WWW.MELBAY.COM

Other Mel Bay Viola Books

Concept and Study for the Viola: The Lobko Method
Modern Viola Method Grade 1 (Norgaard/Scott)
The American Fiddle Method for Viola Vol. 1 (Wicklund/Farr)
American Fiddle Tunes for Solo and Ensemble: Viola/Violin 3 (C. Duncan)
Celtic Fiddle Tunes for Solo and Ensemble: Viola/Violin 3 (C. Duncan)
Christmas Songs for Beginning Viola Level 1 (C. Duncan)
Christmas Strings: Viola/Violin 3 & Ensemble Score (Miller)
Classical Repertoire for Viola Vol. 1 (Puscoiu)
Easy Classics for Viola (Spitzer)
Easy Solos for Beginning Viola (C. Duncan)
Fiddling Classics for Solo & Ensemble: Viola/Violin 3 and Score (C. Duncan)
Fiddle Tunes for Two Violas (Phillips)
Fun with the Viola (W. Bay)
Hymns for Viola Made Easy (Clarke)
Jazz Viola Wizard Junior, Book 1 (Norgaard)
Jazz Viola Wizard Junior, Book 2 (Norgaard)
Music from Around the World for Solo & Ensemble: Viola/Violin 3 (Miller)
My Very Best Christmas: Viola (Khanagov)
Sacred Melodies for Solo Viola (C. Duncan)
Scottish Airs and Dances for Viola & Cello/or Solo Viola (Witt)
Scottish Fiddling for Viola (Witt)
Student's Book of Rounds: Viola (Worth)
The Student Violist: Bach (C. Duncan)
The Student Violist: Beethoven (C. Duncan)
The Student Violist: Handel (C. Duncan)
The Student Violist: Mozart (C. Duncan)
Wedding Music for Solo Viola (Curatolo)
Beginner Viola Theory for Children Book 1 (M. Smith)
Beginner Viola Theory for Children Book 2 (M. Smith)
Beginner Viola Theory for Children Book 3 (M. Smith)
Speed Reading for Viola (Bauer)
Viola Wall Chart (Norgaard)

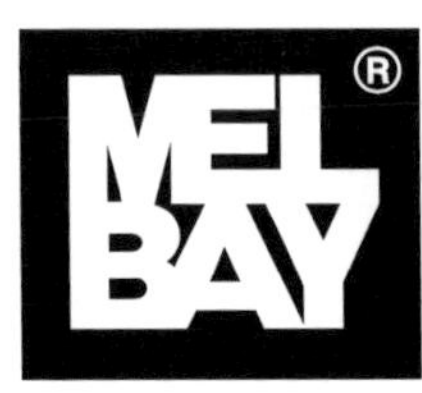

WWW.MELBAY.COM